NAFSA's Guide to
International Partnerships

DEVELOPING SUSTAINABLE ACADEMIC COLLABORATIONS

NAFSA's Guide to
International Partnerships

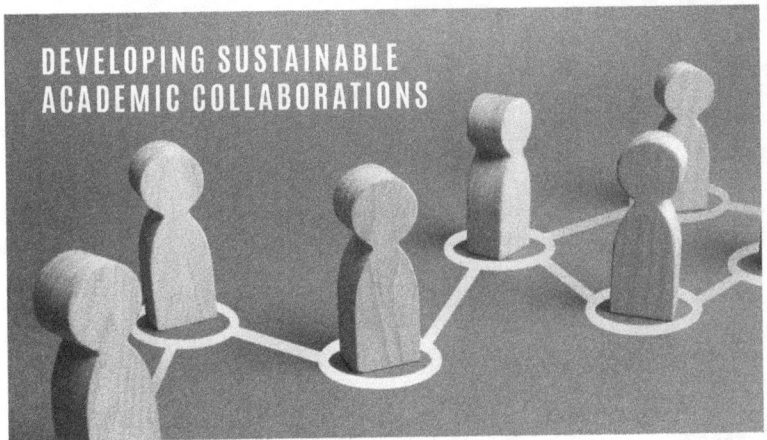

DEVELOPING SUSTAINABLE
ACADEMIC COLLABORATIONS

Edited by **JANE GATEWOOD**

NAFSA

NAFSA's Guide to International Partnerships: Developing Sustainable Academic Collaborations

Edited by Jane Gatewood

NAFSA: Association of International Educators
1307 New York Avenue, NW
8th Floor
Washington, DC 20005-4715

NAFSA is the largest and most comprehensive association of professionals committed to advancing international higher education. Based in the United States, we provide programs, products, services, and a physical and virtual meeting space for the worldwide community of international educators. The association provides leadership to its varied constituencies through establishing principles of good practice and providing professional development opportunities. NAFSA encourages networking among professionals, convenes conferences and collaborative dialogues, and promotes research and knowledge creation to strengthen and serve the field. We lead the way in advocating for a better world through international education.

Cataloging in Publication data are available from the Library of Congress for this book.

ISBN 9781942719359 (print)
ISBN 9781942719380 (ebook)
LCCN 2020934007 (print and ebook)

Edited by Natalie Ngo, NAFSA

BULK PURCHASES
Quantity discounts are available for
workshops and staff development.
Call 1.866.538.1927 to order.

First edition, 2020

10 9 8 7 6 5 4 3 2

Contents

Acknowledgments

would like to thank all the authors who contributed new content to this work. They have provided important perspectives and new practitioner-based content for the field. In addition, several people have provided support and guidance for this volume. I am thankful to them for their work behind the scenes and their dedication. Dorothea Antonio provided the initial suggestion that a book devoted to international partnerships be created, and she provided helpful feedback along the way. Natalie Ngo has been a collaborative and patient editor, prompting and advising as needed along the way. Without them, the project would not have come to fruition. Finally, I would like to recognize the community of practice surrounding international partnerships that has emerged in the field in the last decade—it is an honor to work among such wonderful colleagues.

Foreword

Susan Buck Sutton

NAFSA's Guide to International Partnerships: Developing Sustainable Academic Collaborations stands as a comprehensive, timely, and essential guide to one of the most important changes in the field of international education over the last 2 decades: the growth of international partnerships. Indeed, the increasing emphasis on international partnerships in higher education has been nothing short of remarkable.

When the International Association of Universities (IAU) conducted its first global survey on the state of internationalization among higher education institutions around the world in 2005, enhanced international cooperation was far down on the list of benefits driving greater international work (Knight 2005, 61). In the fifth global survey, however, it emerged as the top-ranked benefit for all regions of the world except North America, where it came in second (Marinoni 2019, 81). And the growing importance of international partnerships even in that region is affirmed by similar surveys conducted by the American Council on Education (ACE). In 2011, 21 percent of U.S. colleges and universities still had no such partnerships, but another 21 percent were starting them for the first time and 48 percent more were intensifying their partnership work (ACE 2012, 31). ACE's 2016 survey showed another 13 percent had taken the plunge into international cooperation (Helms and Brajkovic 2017, 12).

This move from the periphery of academic internationalization to the center reflects a growing recognition of the power of high-performing international partnerships. Once seen as a minor tactic, they have been repositioned as vital to the level of collaboration now needed for authentic global learning, cutting-edge research, professional practice, the rethinking of institutional missions for an interconnected world, and the development of global solutions to global problems. Partnerships can be an essential tool for advancing all of the other goals of academic internationalization. They can also be seen as a goal in and of themselves, generating the insight, transformation, and connectedness needed for higher education institutions to navigate the twenty-first century.

Because this repositioning of international partnerships is so new, however, we are still very much in the midst of defining how we think about them and how we build them. The most recent ACE survey reveals that only 19 percent of U.S. colleges and universities have articulated a formal strategy for partnership development, although another 23 percent are in the process of doing so (Helms and Brajkovic 2017, 12). Adding to this situation, the staff who manage student mobility partnerships are often separate from those who manage partnerships related to research and other types of academic program collaboration. Relatively few institutions have a comprehensive inventory that includes all of their formal institutional agreements and their respective levels of activity.

It is time to address this situation. *NAFSA's Guide to International Partnerships* is a reference manual for the kind of rethinking and reorganization needed to advance partnerships at institutions of all types. It provides detailed, almost encyclopedic frameworks for understanding and building the wide variety of partnerships now emerging, elaborating on the benefits and challenges of each.

These frameworks are the result of asking the authors of each chapter to focus on the general principles of a particular aspect of partnership strategy and development. The authors draw on deep experience with international partnerships at their own institutions. Examples and case studies are woven into their accounts. The focus, however, is on the general lessons that these experiences yield and their connection to our emerging understanding of partnership work. Each chapter derives power from its placement with the others, and together they create a comprehensive picture of the key elements of international partnership work.

In creating this broad view, the volume places discussions on partnerships for student mobility next to those for research and community engagement. The ways in which each enhances the other emerge, as does the concept of "comprehensive" partnerships that span these types. This thorough discussion of partnership models and types is complemented by other chapters that dive into the considerations involved in setting up an accepted and effective partnership approval and tracking process, as well as qualitative principles and quantitative criteria for assessing the health and impact of existing linkages.

Several overarching themes thread through these eight chapters, creating another level of connection and insight. Perhaps the most important of these is the necessity of an institution-wide approach to partnership development. Although it plays an important role in catalyzing and supporting linkages, the international office must not be the only locus for this work. Strong partnerships emerge out of the entire ecosystem of international collaboration in which an institution participates, both locally and beyond its national borders.

Linkages formalized by institutional memoranda of understanding (MOUs) intersect with and should support the institution's larger mission and international strategy, from individual faculty research projects to the home countries of its international students to the sister-city relationships of its surrounding community. Neither narrowly top-down nor narrowly bottom-up approaches are sufficient. And those who aim to build good institutional partnerships must navigate both extremes by inviting broad participation in a process seen as both legitimate and important.

The international partnerships of today vary from and operate on a different landscape from those of a few decades ago. Student exchanges, often taken as the default definition of international partnerships in the past, are no longer dominant—and those that exist often take a different shape from their predecessors. It is time to pool our collective wisdom to enter confidently and effectively into this new territory, and that is precisely what this volume does.

References

American Council on Education (ACE). 2012. *Mapping Internationalization on U.S. Campuses: 2012 Edition.* Washington DC: American Council on Education.

Helms, Robin, and Lucia Brajkovic. 2017. *Mapping Internationalization on U.S. Campuses: 2017 Edition.* Washington DC: American Council on Education.

Knight, Jane. 2005. *Internationalization of Higher Education: New Directions, New Challenges.* International Association of Universities Global Survey Report. Paris: IAU Secretariat – UNESCO House.

Marinoni, Giorgio. 2019. *Internationalization of Higher Education: An Evolving Landscape, Locally and Globally.* International Association of Universities 5th Global Survey. Berlin: DUZ Academic Publishers.

Introduction

Jane Gatewood

nternational partnerships serve as fundamental tools for international engagement. These partnerships help institutions in the process of internationalizing their academic curricula, research, and service—from amplifying the capacity for teaching and research to injecting international dimensions into degree and study programs. When developed and used effectively, partnerships can support comprehensive international programs, research, and global engagement, allowing institutions to maximize their strengths while also closing gaps and deepening connections abroad. Partnerships enable institutions to do more with less by building on comparative strengths and utilizing complementary resources. As with any tool, partnerships can do these things only if designed and implemented with focus and vision.

The Global Landscape

Emerging as elements of increasing importance over the last decade, institutional partnerships serve as both an internationalization tool and a function of the international higher education landscape. The American Council on Education (ACE)'s (2012) *Mapping Internationalization on U.S. Campuses* charts the emergence of institutional partnerships as key features of internationalization on U.S. campuses—with partnerships following only traditional mobility schemas such as study abroad and recruiting international students in prominence. The trends of increased focus on partnerships continued in ACE's 2017 installment of *Mapping Internationalization on U.S. Campuses* (Helms and Brajkovic 2017).

The European Association for International Education produced similar findings, noting that the development and implementation of international partnerships makes up one of the key trends in internationalization (Sandström and Weimer 2016). The Association of International Education Administrators (AIEA)'s 2014 and 2017 surveys of senior international officers (SIOs) demonstrated parallel trends: the 2014 survey found that approximately half of responding institutions had begun to develop or expand partnerships in recent years, and one-third reported having a staff member dedicated to partnership development. Both the 2014 and 2017 AIEA surveys ranked partnerships as one of the top three topics for SIOs.

These trends toward institutional prioritization of partnership development are likely informed by various pressures from both policy and economic standpoints, since various governments and funding agencies around the world have made calls for increased collaborations, efficiencies, and innovation. The European Union offers awards for Erasmus+ Strategic Partnerships, which are defined as "transnational projects designed to develop and share innovative practices, promote cooperation, peer learning, and exchanges" (European Commission 2020). Similarly, the National Science Foundation (NSF) has had numerous iterations of funding schemes to promote international collaboration (e.g., the Partnerships for International Research and Education), most of which are managed through NSF's Office of International Science and Engineering. These funding schemes are often matched by other governments around the world in collective partnership to advance innovation and education. Significantly too, the final goal of the United Nations's (2015) Sustainable Development Goals—number 17—calls for global partnership for sustainable development.

International Partnerships

While partnerships have the component parts of service-related tools or instruments, they also operate in a behavioral space of organizational relationships; like any relationship, they must be stewarded and, at times, curated. Just as an individual likely cannot have hundreds of close friends, an institution likely cannot sustain hundreds of successful, meaningful partnerships. In sum, partnerships cannot and should not be measured by the mere number of contracts or agreements.

While the two are related, the mere existence of a contract does not necessarily equate to the existence of an active, beneficial partner relationship. This faulty equivalence, though, has been prevalent across the field of international higher education, leading many institutions to tout the sheer number of agreements as evidence of global connections and engagement. An international partnership, simply put, involves at least two entities with different contexts and cultures working together to achieve mutually defined and mutually beneficial goals and objectives. While this may seem straightforward, managing relationships across cultures and institutional contexts requires considerable planning and finesse.

Just as the myth that agreements and partnerships are synonymous has prevailed in the field, other myths often surround the discourse of international partnership development and can undercut success. For instance, some colleagues may assume that partnerships should be "uncomplicated," often meaning institutions should just sign a contract and move forward with the collaboration. While striving for effortless and efficient partner engagement should be a goal of any partnership manager, navigating this terrain is often complex and, at times, quite complicated. Achieving trust, one of the core tenets of a productive partnership, involves both short-term and long-term investments of time, resources, and patience.

Additionally, institutions often operate under the assumption that high-level leadership visits serve to ignite long-lasting relationships, but, depending on the culture of the institutions, this may or may not be the case. Institutions that operate in a deeply hierarchical and centralized fashion may benefit from this theory, but those with stronger traditions of responsibility-centered management and faculty governance will not. Partnership managers need to understand their institutions well and be able to translate organizational behavior to their partners effectively in order to cultivate successful relationships.

Engagement Frameworks

The partner engagement framework in figure 1 provides a structure for interpreting institutional culture as it relates to international partnerships, revealing the pros and cons of different contexts—from top-down to bottom-up cultivation strategies and from a portfolio of numerous formal partners to a select few.

Figure 1. Partner Engagement Framework

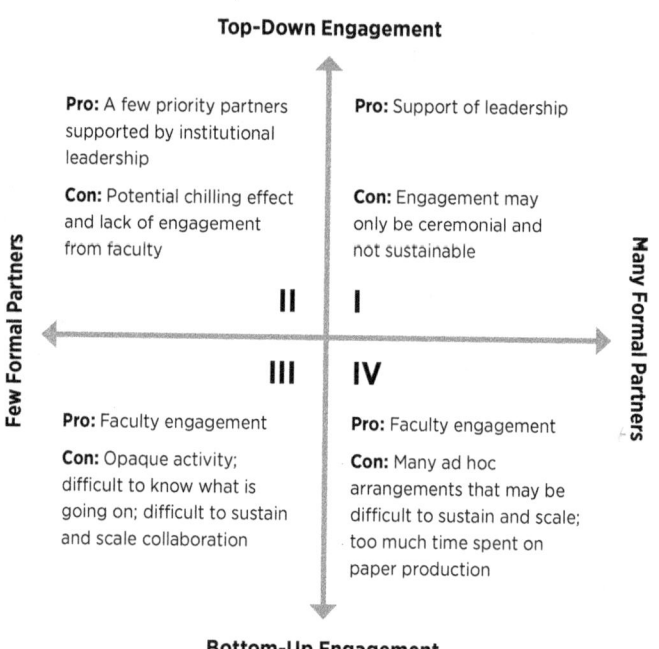

Institutions can use this framework to identify not only where they presently are in their partnership development strategy, but also where they want to go. For instance, an institution that is currently positioned in quadrant I (highly top-down with many formal partners) will have to guard against purely ceremonial engagement, while continuing to cultivate the support of leadership. Correspondingly, leaders of internationalization and partnership managers may have to shift the balance of engagement by involving more faculty in a few partnerships that will continue to have the support of leadership.

Conversely, an institution in quadrant III (bottom-up engagement with few formal partners) may struggle to reflect accurately the depth of institutional connections, while also benefiting from considerable faculty collaboration. In order to have better institutional insight into international engagement, SIOs and partnership managers will likely need to employ strategies to uncover and elevate these institutional connections.

Whatever the organizational structure and objectives, institutional international partnerships have emerged as a primary component of comprehensive internationalization strategies. International partnerships support institutions as they diversify their educational offerings, amplify their research portfolios, augment their corporate engagement strategies, and extend the impact of their service. Higher education institutions have long collaborated with one another for both teaching and research. But in the age of globalization, with its core research challenges and increased student demand, institutions are now positioning themselves to collaborate for the long term as effectively and efficiently as possible.

Overview of the Book

Keeping with the demands of these trends, *NAFSA's Guide to International Partnerships: Developing Sustainable Academic Collaborations* delves into the parameters of international partnerships, identifying sound practices for the cultivation of partnerships that foster deep, rich, and sustainable connections internationally. Led by a group of international education professionals representing a variety of institutions from across the North America, the chapters in this volume cover a broad spectrum of partnership types, modes, and means of engagement, as well as methods of assessing, scaling, and sustaining them institutionally.

The chapters reflect practitioner perspectives, and the authors have proven experience in their respective domains of partner engagement and development. In addition, many of the chapters contain figures and tables illustrating various concepts and structures to assist readers in conceptualizing sound practices. Readers may use this volume as a tool to help them develop and assess their own institutional structures or as a guide for developing effective future practices.

Chapter Features

The book is divided into roughly two sections. The first portion, comprising chapters 2 through 5, considers components and practicalities associated with a variety of partnership types, with a chapter each dedicated to educational mobility, research collaborations, and community engagement. Chapter 1 offers a deep dive into the dimensions and dynamics of international partnerships, providing definitions and operating principles for partnerships. Chad Hoseth and Shehan Thampapillai explore various motivations for numerous partnership types. In a compelling turn, they draw a parallel between partnering in the higher education space and collaborations that occur in nature, noting importantly that not all forms of engagement are positive. Institutions and partnership managers will want to pay careful attention to these types and points as they develop their own institutional frameworks and practices.

In chapter 2, Kalpen Trivedi covers the partnership category likely most familiar to the higher education community: partnerships for educational mobility. Trivedi's framing historicizes the tradition of educational mobility, exchange, and study abroad, demonstrating that while this partnership type may have a long tradition dating back centuries, it continues to reinvent itself by adapting to student and institutional demands. He further introduces a theme other chapters will echo: the importance of understanding and working effectively within one's own institutional culture. Trivedi stresses the importance of building internal connections to ensure that external engagement is well supported at home.

Outlining the specifics of international research partnerships, Kiki Caruson provides essential tactics for identifying existing research connections in chapter 3. She discusses strategies ranging from reviewing publications and faculty annual reports to working with the sponsored research office to understand connections made via external grants and funding. Caruson shows that by reviewing information and data related to an institution's research portfolio, international leaders and partnership managers can draw on existing connections to build robust institutional collaborations rooted in faculty research priorities and expertise.

Jöel Gallegos picks up the thread of building connections at home in chapter 4, which focuses on community-engaged international partnerships. Gallegos advances the argument for internationalization at home by demonstrating what can be accomplished on campus through relationships with the local community that are carefully cultivated for the long term. He also illustrates that community-engaged partnerships can help foster broad-based community connections globally via networks, associations, and key programming.

Chapter 5 seeks to bring the various themes established in the previous chapters together in a segment focused on comprehensive partnerships. Defined as those cultivated for the long term between institutions, comprehensive institutional partnerships hold numerous possibilities when they span disciplinary boundaries, involve many stakeholders, and have multiple modes of engagement.

Marking the second portion of the book, chapter 6 shifts to institutional case studies. In a segment devoted to partnerships with corporate entities and the nonprofit sector, Paul Allen Miller presents examples from the University of South Carolina. These examples reveal the opportunities that exist for institutions that align their academic and research connections abroad with the economic development and other priorities of their locales. The chapter provides a useful descriptive model that other institutions will likely seek to emulate.

Chapter 7 examines an aspect of partner development that can often be fraught and time-intensive for institutions just starting to develop a partnership strategy. Focused on negotiating, reviewing, and curating partnership agreements, this chapter provides a replicable example of an agreement management process employed at the University of California, Davis. Joanna Regulska, Jolynn Shoemaker, and Elizabeth Landridge-Noti describe an institutional process for managing agreement development and review that includes faculty members while also adhering to statewide protocols at a large public research institution.

The volume closes with a case study from the University of Calgary focused on partnership assessment. Illustrating an award-winning practice and tool kit developed at UCalgary—the International Partnership Assessment Rating Index (IPARI)—Janaka Ruwanpura and colleagues demonstrate the value of creating a robust assessment tool early in the institutional process for partnership development. The UCalgary example suggests that a robust assessment process can help institutions map where they want to go and assess how they are progressing on their journey. The IPARI framework has many adaptable facets for use at other institutions of varying types.

Each chapter presents a unique perspective on international partnerships. From establishing a common vocabulary and typologies to providing replicable assessment tools and management frameworks, each segment advances the professional discourse surrounding international higher education partnerships. While in many ways international collaboration is as old as higher education itself, this volume illustrates that considerable work and progress is being made in the domain of international partnerships. Designed for senior leaders of internationalization and for partnership managers alike, the volume provides new voices and perspectives on the development and management of productive, sustainable international partnerships.

References

American Council on Education (ACE). 2012. *Mapping Internationalization on U.S. Campuses: 2012 Edition.* Washington, DC: American Council on Education. https://www.acenet.edu/Documents/Mapping-Internationalizationon-US-Campuses-2012-full.pdf.

Association of International Education Administrators (AIEA). 2014. "A Survey on Senior International Education Officers, Their Institutions and Offices." Durham, NC: Association of International Education Administrators. https://www.aieaworld.org/assets/docs/Surveys/sio%20survey%20summary.pdf.

Association of International Education Administrators (AIEA). 2017. "The SIO Profile: A Preliminary Analysis of the Survey on Senior International Education Officers, Their Institutions and Offices." Durham, NC: Association of International Education Administrators. https://www.aieaworld.org/assets/docs/Surveys/final-2017%20executive%20summary_sio%20profile%20survey.pdf.

European Commission. 2020. "Strategic Partnerships." European Commission. https://ec.europa.eu/programmes/erasmus-plus/opportunities/strategic-partnerships-field-education-training-and-youth_en.

Helms, Robin Matross, and Lucia Brajkovic. 2017. *Mapping Internationalization on U.S. Campuses: 2017 Edition.* Washington, DC: American Council on Education. https://www.acenet.edu/Documents/Mapping-Internationalization-2017.pdf.

Sandström, Anna-Malin, and Leasa Weimer. 2016. "International Strategic Partnerships." *EAIE Barometer.* European Association for International Education. https://www.eaie.org/our-resources/library/publication/Research-and-trends/international-strategic-partnerships.html.

United Nations. 2015. *Transforming Our World: The 2030 Agenda for Sustainable Development.* United Nations. https://sustainabledevelopment.un.org/post2015/transformingourworld.

1

International Partnership Dynamics and Types

Chad Hoseth and Shehan Thampapillai

International partnerships help enable higher education institutions to achieve their strategic internationalization goals—although those motivations may differ across institutional types and borders. The objectives for comprehensive international engagement through partnerships may include education abroad opportunities, international student enrollment, faculty productivity in an international setting, institutional branding, academic reputation, alumni engagement, service, and beyond; the priority standing of these various goals may differ significantly between institutions. Nonetheless, institutions worldwide have begun to place a high value on the development of international partnerships with other institutions that are cultivated for the long-term, strategic aims of each institution.

To engage in the global marketplace and to offer their students, staff, and faculty new cross-cultural opportunities, institutions often sign a variety of agreements, including memoranda of understanding (MOUs), with partner institutions worldwide. However, general agreements and MOUs often do little more than fill file cabinets precisely because of a lack of specific, achievable goals for the partnerships. Institutions that are unable to articulate their objectives definitively may have a large number of ineffective MOUs and nascent collaborations, resulting in minimal international engagement. Instead of focusing on paper-based agreements as the object of their international partnership strategy, institutions should carefully define their desired outcomes for global engagement in order to identify the most applicable partnership types and determine the characteristics to look for in their partner institutions.

This chapter seeks to introduce international partnerships in two ways. First, the chapter examines different characteristics and dynamics of partnerships. Second, it provides a broad overview of some of the different types of activities that are included in international partnerships at higher education institutions. Understanding these foundational partnership dynamics and activities can help institutions find the right fit for their needs in order to build the foundation for successful and sustainable institutional relationships.

Partnerships and Agreements

The words "partnership" and "agreement" can create some confusion for international educators because they are often used interchangeably. However, agreements on their own are not partnerships. Agreements are the written instruments that institutions use to delineate the specific goals of an international partnership; a well-crafted agreement should outline the rules, mitigate risk, assign responsible parties, and set forth an action plan for engagement. The text written in an agreement should include the names of the responsible parties, timelines, acknowledgment of resource commitments, and a clear illustration of what the partners intend to accomplish together. At best, agreements are manifestations of, and frameworks for, partnerships; but on their own, they do not constitute partnerships. This chapter attends to the specifics related to partnership development and management, rather than the particulars of agreement management.

International Partnerships

International partnerships are active collaborations developed for the long term between two or more institutions or entities from different contexts and cultures that work together for shared goals and outcomes, including student learning, scholarly achievement, and other initiatives of interest. Partnerships can exist between institutions of higher education, as well as with the public, private, and nongovernmental sectors. Institutions may choose to assign categories to their international partnerships, such as formal, informal, strategic, multidisciplinary, and other classifications. This chapter uses a broad lens when considering partnerships, but with a bias toward active partnerships intended to achieve tangible outcomes and long-term engagement.

Under a "what gets counted, counts" approach, a desire to place a high value on the number of MOUs in place often exists, regardless of whether the partnerships are active or inactive. These ceremonial MOUs may have been signed by administrators or faculty who left the institution some time ago, and the content of the MOUs may include little reference to the actual intentions or plans that led to the development of the agreements in the first place. As a result, some institutions may focus their attention on the quantity of partnership agreements signed, believing in the notion that a larger number of agreements suggests a higher level of internationalization. However, these MOUs are not likely to produce concrete results and often become dormant or unsustainable in the long term. In order to develop effective global relationships, institutions should first establish their objectives and goals, which then inform the type and dynamics of each partnership. These decisions govern the language of the agreement and the partnering institution that is approached.

Partnership Dynamics

International partnerships can help institutions engage in a remarkable array of activities. As a result, institutions benefit from understanding the basic dynamics of partnerships, which can allow them to move forward in a thoughtful and intentional manner. The initial definition of an international partnership—two or more institutions or entities with different contexts and cultures working together for shared goals and outcomes—brings to mind other types of partnerships occurring in the natural world, for example animals and plants whose coexistence produces food, shelter, and protection for the other (e.g., bees whose pursuit of nectar helps to pollinate flowers and transmit seeds). Ecologically speaking, these naturally occurring relationships are mutualistic—the relationships operate through varying levels of cooperation, or symbiosis, that produce beneficial results for each party. Since the natural world provides a framework for considering some basic forms and goals of partnerships, applying these same fundamental dynamics to international partnerships can help institutions build enduring collaborations. By extending this metaphor to the world of international higher education, it is possible to delineate various types of mutualistic relationships, or partnerships, that occur in this space.

Symbiotic mutualism, whereby both partners benefit from the relationship, provides the best example of a framework for productive institutional partnerships due to its win-win outcomes. However, partnership managers should be aware that other types of symbiosis can occur in the international education environment as well. In parasitic relationships, one party benefits while the other suffers. In commensal relationships, one party benefits while the other garners no benefit. The goal for most international partnerships, though, is a mutualistic, symbiotic relationship.

While scientific literature further characterizes the different forms of mutualistic relationships as trophic (relationships that provide an equal exchange of resources), defensive (relationships that provide a service for protection), and dispersive (relationships that exchange a service or support for a resource) (Schupp, Jordano, and Gómez 2017), for this discussion of international partnership dynamics, these varietals are redefined based on their functional attributes:

- Resource-based partnerships, which are rooted in the reciprocal exchange of like resources;

- Support-based partnerships, which are driven by access needs or goals; and

- Complementary partnerships, which allow for a dynamic interplay of benefits between the partners.

The subsequent sections examine key components of the different typologies to help partnership managers interpret the underlying dynamics and attributes of international collaborations, as well as develop effective practices to support such relationships. International partnerships have emerged as a fundamental component of the international higher education ecosystem.

Resource-Based Partnerships

Resource-based partnerships involve an equal benefit to both partners because each institution exchanges similar resources, as in the case of bilateral student exchanges and the exchange of faculty academic and research appointments (discussed in more detail later). This partnership dynamic is ideally suited for institutions that seek to exchange an equal number and type of resources. In order for such relationships to succeed, prospective partners should have a shared vision and similar institutional commitment, synergies in academic and research portfolios, and confirmed participation interest among the target cohorts.

Even though the operating principle of equal reciprocity typically creates a revenue-neutral scenario for most institutions, the success of resource-based partnerships is largely dependent upon institutional buy-in and support because partnering institutions must agree to work together to share resources. Since institutional priorities drive institutional commitment, and since institutional culture underpins organizational behavior, institutions that face significant deltas from their partners in these domains may confront challenges in partnership feasibility and sustainability. Assessing organizational priorities, commitment, and culture early in the partnership development trajectory is, thus, an essential step in establishing resource-based partnerships.

An equally important contributor to the success of resource-based partnerships is synergy between the partners' academic and research portfolios, both in terms of operational alignment and participant interest. From the perspective of bilateral student exchanges, the desired outcome is uninterrupted progress toward the degree for students studying abroad, and this is affected by transfer credit for studies taken at the partner institution. For this form of reciprocity to work, both institutions need to offer a comparable curriculum in similar areas of academic study. Significant overlap in the curriculum may even lead to discussions about collaborative degrees or other joint programming.

This condition of academic comparability applies to academic and research exchanges of faculty members as well; if visiting scholars are to teach short courses, shadow lectures, or undertake research at the partner institution, then academic and research areas must be well aligned. Thus, syllabi, course catalogs, grants awarded, and publication outputs can serve as elements for assessing the viability of resource-based faculty- and student-oriented partnership success.

Correspondingly, interest level among the target audiences of resource-based partnerships must be estimated, particularly given the core operational principle of equal reciprocity—exchanging like for like. Even when other characteristics are met, if interest from the target cohort lags at either partner institution, the resource-based exchange will be difficult to sustain.

Support-Based Partnerships

Not all partnerships involve an equal sharing of resources. Under support-based partnerships, one partner benefits from access to new opportunities in exchange for providing in-country support, service, or resources. This type of partnership is ideally suited for in-country program delivery and offerings by a foreign provider, such as some forms of collaborative degrees, overseas offices and branch campuses, and noncredit training and multinational research programs (discussed in more detail later).

In many countries, regulatory frameworks and other legal restrictions allow foreign institutions to offer in-country programs only via partnerships with local providers. With support-based partnerships, the in-country (host) partner provides legal or other means for operation and the foreign partner provides a service, such as access to a new program, to the host partner. It is important to note that host country regulations often inform in-country delivery of training programs, clinical trials, and development work, and, in such cases, host country regulations operate *in addition* to those of the home country. Thus, support-based partnerships involve different considerations and communication models than resource-based partnerships because the support and resources that are exchanged are rather specific to the in-country infrastructure and regulations.

For support-based partnerships, trust is paramount because if the in-country partner does not meet its commitments, the foreign institution's ability to operate in the host country would cease. Equally, if the foreign partner does not deliver its programs as planned, the local institution may suffer enrollment declines or other losses. For this reason, institutional stability, consistent leadership, and the partner's in-country networks all play a major role in ensuring that the associated risks can be managed.

A support-based partnership can easily transition into a parasitic relationship due to a lack of trust between institutions and a failure to meet commitments. If, for example, a foreign institution's program is replicated by the in-country partner and offered as part of that partner's academic portfolio, this will undermine the original transnational program offered via the support-based partnership. This problematic situation could be addressed through a robust agreement or, in cases where the agreement is breached, litigation. However, the challenges and costs associated with such strategies can be significant and, for these reasons, are often not viable options.

Institutions seeking support-based relationships should take care to ensure the strength and stability of their relationships, just as they take care to craft the actionable agreements. Institutional stability and a historical trend of consistent leadership can provide a strong foundation for support-based relationships. When there are frequent changes in institutional leadership, it may become more difficult for the original intentions of the partnership to be carried forward. New personnel may bring in different visions and directions for both the institution and its partnerships, which could potentially lead to altered or dormant agreements. On the other hand, previous experience working together helps to build that trust between partners and align the priorities of the partnership, which can help institutional partnerships weather leadership transitions.

Institutions will also want to work with partners that have strong connections and extensive networks in the host countries because tapping into these resources can help the foreign institution's programs or services receive more positive acceptance in-country. Fundamentally, in support-based partnerships, a foreign institution is building on the local reputation and connections of the partner institution to deliver on its goals in-country. Thus, choosing a partner that has a positive reputation can lead to a smoother approval process from local government bodies and help maximize opportunities—in some cases leading to in-country funding and support. With successful support-based partnerships, one connection can open the door to opportunities in new, untapped markets because the collaborative groundwork has been established effectively.

Complementary Partnerships

Combining elements present in resource-based and support-based partnerships, a complementary partnership is built on the premise that one institution receives something (a service, a payment) for providing a supportive resource (access, permissions) to the other, thereby establishing a resource-service dynamic. Complementary partnerships are ideal for institutions that have a knowledge gap or lack of resources or networks that they are looking to supplement through a partnership.

Twinning programs, some collaborative degree programs, online courses, and academic curricular exchanges operate under a complementary partnership model, as do some research and development programs (discussed in more detail later). For example, two partner institutions agree to engage in a transnational consecutive degree or twinning program whereby Partner A originates students who will ultimately graduate from Partner B; in this case, Partner A provides a resource (students) and Partner B provides a service (teaching).

Additionally, international research and development projects often operate under a complementary framework because it grants the foreign institution access to particular scenarios, situations, or paradigms unavailable in the home country, often in exchange for in-country training and development of local students, staff, faculty, or facilities. For example, Partner A may be seeking to offer a specialization in a niche area that is not currently within its academic portfolio. Rather than trying to recruit an expert in this particular niche, the knowledge gap can be closed through a partnership with Partner B, which already has faculty on staff in this specialty area who can assist with curriculum development and guest teaching. In this instance, the service would be Partner B's intellectual property and the resource would be the financial benefit provided by Partner A for services rendered.

For a complementary relationship to succeed, prospective partners should have differences or gaps between their respective academic portfolios and research specializations, as well as transparency and openness because these relationships are more effective when the assets and attributes of the one complement the other. An institution is more likely to enter into a collaborative degree partnership if the program being offered adds value to, and does not compete with, its own academic portfolio. Furthermore, because complementary partnerships involve the combining of resources and services, partnering institutions need to be willing to have their practices and staff evaluated by the partner institution. A reluctance to permit this level of transparency can undo a complementary twinning arrangement. Transparency between partner institutions can be encouraged by adopting a narrative that focuses on helping the partner rather than assessing institutional practices.

Given that a complementary partnership does not provide an equal return for each partner, both partners must be comfortable with the parameters and understand the total benefits that are generated from the partnership. These relationships require institutions to recognize their own curricular and research gaps and identify partners that can balance their portfolios in other ways. Similar to resource-based partnerships, complementary partnerships require support from institutional leadership in order to combine resources, and they rely on active interest among the target cohorts. As with support-based partnership models, each partner in a complementary relationship needs to trust that the other will meet its obligations ethically and effectively; otherwise the program, the students, and the partner institutions may be negatively affected. Taking elements that characterize the other two dynamics, complementary partnerships contribute toward institutional internationalization goals by bridging gaps and extending capacity.

The dynamics between partnering institutions can affect the organization, implementation, results, and sustainability of the relationship. Whether they are engaging in resource-based, support-based, or complementary partnerships, both institutions must clearly establish their expectations and desired outcomes. The partners must also assess their own institutional culture and motivations for engaging with a particular partner to establish and assess the more ephemeral question of "fit." Productive relationships are developed through ongoing, realistic communication and assessment between partners, which can help to build trust and consistency, two of the most important elements of international partnerships.

Partnership Types

A wide range of partnership types exists, each one involving different levels of infrastructure, resources, engagement, and benefits. The specific goals that both institutions outline for the relationship should directly correspond to the type of partnership selected. The following sections provide overviews of a range of international partnership activities involving student learning opportunities, international student enrollment opportunities, faculty opportunities, and other strategic institutional opportunities, many of which will receive more detailed attention in the other chapters of this book.

Partnerships for Student Learning

Institutions often develop partnerships to enhance their portfolio of programs that allow students to take their education abroad. Below are just a few of the most common outbound student opportunities available.

Bilateral Student Exchanges

Bilateral student exchanges are among the more popular and widely used partnership activities in higher education. In a typical bilateral student exchange model, students from one institution go to study at the other institution for a designated period of time, while, often simultaneously, students from the second institution live and study at the first institution. Students register for courses at the partner institution but pay for the tuition at their home institution. This model provides students with a quality international experience at a lower cost than many other models. However, the financial balance that is required of the two institutions can make bilateral student exchange agreements more challenging to sustain over the long term. If the bilateral flow of students turns into a one-way flow for an extended period of time, the exchange agreement will fall out of balance and become difficult to sustain.

To manage the relationship, officials from partnering institutions often meet regularly, at conferences and through in-person visits, exchanging updates on their respective institutions and curricula. Institutions often engage in regular assessment of academic offerings to ensure that the programs align with the needs of the participating students. As a result, a smooth credit transfer process between the two institutions is usually established. Additionally, this partnership model facilitates a more stable stream of students between the partner institutions, allowing for enhanced academic and nonacademic services for the participating students. Bilateral student exchanges can systematize student support efforts at the host institution, such as housing for international students, and more fully integrate students into the campus community.

Experiential Programs

International collaborations between partnering institutions can improve and extend opportunities for student learning in other ways, including service learning, field experience, and research. Partnerships can provide sustained and structured access to different communities, academic and research facilities, faculty instruction, and many other services that can enhance students' academic and professional experiences globally. Institutional partnerships that establish experiential programs can require more preparatory work and institutional oversight than other models, such as using private sector providers. However, partnerships can minimize participation costs for students and increase institutional engagement in program development for the benefit of the students.

International Student Enrollment Opportunities

International student enrollment is another major area of interest for higher education institutions, and partnerships have contributed to innovations and increases in student mobility and student enrollment. A number of partnership activities can support degree-seeking student enrollment on campuses, ranging from collaborative degrees to online programs.

Collaborative Degrees

The number of collaborative degree programs has been steadily on the rise in recent years as many institutions seek to enhance their global reputations and internationalization portfolios by linking with other institutions in key academic areas. Partnering for such programs enable institutions to diversify their curricula, student body, and faculty relationships. Collaborative degree options include:

- Dual and double degrees, which result in two degrees at the same academic level (e.g., one master's degree from Partner A and one master's degree from Partner B); the degrees can be exactly the same (double), e.g., two MBAs, or similar (dual), e.g., one MBA and one MSc;

- Consecutive degrees, which result in two separate degrees at two different levels (e.g., one bachelor's degree from Partner A and one master's degree from Partner B); and

- Joint degrees, which result in one degree jointly conferred by two partner institutions (e.g., one master's degree from Partner A and Partner B).

DUAL AND DOUBLE DEGREES

Dual degrees and double degrees allow students to gain two academic degrees at the same level from two partner institutions, often via consolidated admission requirements and condensed programs of study. A dual- or double-degree program involves a student studying at the home institution for an established period of time and then transferring to the partner institution for a similar established period of time. The student earns two degrees at the same academic level, one from each institution, over a shorter span of time than it would take to earn the degrees consecutively. For example, Simon Fraser University in British Columbia, Canada, and Zhejiang University in Hangzhou, China, have partnered to offer a dual degree in computing science, with participating students earning a bachelor's degree from each institution (for more information, visit www.sfu.ca/computing/prospective-students/undergraduate-students/programs/degree-programs/dual-degree-program.html). Dual- and double-degree programs can be designed to focus on undergraduate education (often called 2+2 and 3+1 programs), serve as a bridge between an undergraduate and graduate program, or focus exclusively on graduate studies (often called 1+1 programs).

However, at some institutions, especially those in the United States, the academic requirements that affect transfer credit can impede domestic students from participating in these programs to the same degree as international students. Dual and double degrees have also earned some sceptics, as some international education thought leaders have highlighted the dilemmas inherent in these types of collaborative degrees, including issues surrounding completion requirements, certification, and the legitimacy of qualifications (Knight 2011). Dual and double degrees have also been called into question as being "two for the cost of one," with the double counting of course credits an issue that merits further consideration (Knight and Lee 2012). Institutions need to be mindful of these concerns as they structure curriculum and transfer schemas.

CONSECUTIVE DEGREES

Consecutive degrees result in students receiving two full degrees at two different levels from two partner institutions. Under a partnership agreement, two institutions may establish an integrated program that allows participating students to receive their bachelor's degrees from their home institution and then their master's degrees from the partner institution abroad. For example, The University of Georgia (UGA) in Athens, Georgia, and Istanbul Technical University (ITU) in Istanbul, Turkey, have developed a collaborative bachelor's/master's degree program in landscape architecture (see international.uga.edu/data/partnerships-map). Participating students complete 3 years of study at ITU and then attend 2 years of study at UGA, earning a bachelor's degree from ITU and a master's degree from UGA.

Such linkages can help feed graduate programs by developing strong pipelines between undergraduate and graduate institutions. By developing these consecutive linkages, institutions with strong undergraduate programs can encourage the continued academic success of their graduates through progressive enrollment in a partner's master's degree program. In such a complementary partnership model, institutions that lack graduate or other specialized programs can build on the offerings of partners, and the partners offering graduate study are able to depend upon a steady stream of well-prepared students from the undergraduate partner.

JOINT DEGREES

For a joint degree, the partner institutions work together to develop a single degree curriculum and jointly confer one degree and diploma to the participating students. This might result, for example, in a single diploma with both institutions' names and logos. The most common framework for a joint degree exists in Europe, where collaborative degrees originated. The Erasmus Mundus Joint Master Degree framework provides for consortia-based program and degree delivery across many European countries (for more information, visit ec.europa.eu/programmes/erasmus-plus/opportunities/individuals/students/erasmus-mundus-joint-master-degrees_en). Since the outcome of joint degree programs is one degree, concerns related to credential inflation pose less of a problem for joint degrees than for dual or double degrees.

Joint degrees are complex, requiring a higher level of academic coordination and communication between the partner institutions than with dual or double degrees. Both institutions need to agree on the admissions criteria, admissions procedures, course articulation, tuition and fees, course registration, faculty participation, housing and other logistics, student support, the sharing of official transcripts, and even the language on the final diploma. In some countries, issues around accreditation and academic assessments make joint programs difficult to establish. Additionally, some locales may require that a new legal entity be created between two partner institutions for the diploma to be valid. Despite the time and effort involved, building joint degree programs allows for easy mobility and collaborative credentialing, which can create long-term and sustainable benefits for each institution.

Challenges and Benefits of Collaborative Degrees

The ability to implement a successful collaborative degree program rests heavily on the strength of the relationship between the partnering institutions. Such programs require a great deal of work, communication, and agreement to develop an appropriate level of academic articulation between the two institutions. Academic officials, faculty, and staff in the registrar offices at both institutions must be deeply involved when establishing the academic transfer credit process. Collaborative degree programs also benefit from active engagement from other support offices including academic advising, international student advising, financial aid, student affairs, and housing. Thus, the administrative effort required to establish a collaborative degree academic partnership can be significant.

However, the strong institutional links that are built as the foundation of these programs can attract new populations of students over the long term. In some cases, prospective students can be identified well in advance of their arrival at the second campus, providing more clarity for enrollment managers. From the faculty standpoint, they are often engaged in active, ongoing communication when developing the academic components of the partnerships, which can result in opportunities for additional forms of faculty collaboration. The collaborative degree model offers a pathway for sustained international enrollment over many years and provides participating students with meaningful global educational experiences.

Online Courses

Online instruction provides another model for delivering content in an affordable and convenient manner, and partnerships are beginning to capitalize on these programs in order to reach a larger number of students. For example, the State University of New York (SUNY)'s Collaborative Online International Learning (COIL) Center has partnered with the Latin America Academy to develop team-taught courses for students at SUNY and universities in Latin America, with collaborative student work taking place online (for more information, visit coil.suny.edu/page/coil-latin-america-academy). The SUNY COIL Center has also developed partnerships involving 18 Mexican institutions, 13 SUNY universities and colleges, and four universities outside of New York State, resulting in 39 COIL-embedded courses taught during the 2016–17 academic term (for more information, visit coil.suny.edu/node/251).

Online learning, however, presents its own set of challenges. It can be difficult to develop synchronous courses across different time zones, and asynchronous courses do not include real-time communication between the instructor and participating students. However, when students are able to participate in a synchronous learning environment, advances in video and audio functionality on computing and mobile devices allow for more authentic, real-time interactions.

Online learning allows institutional partners to collaborate on and share educational content with students across the traditional barriers of time and space. In some instances, online instruction can be delivered with an international partner, where the instruction helps augment an academic degree program in another country. For example, at Colorado State University, the department of Human Dimensions of Natural Resources offers a master's degree in tourism management to cohorts of students at Central China Normal University in Wuhan, China (see source.colostate.edu/csu-online-welcomes-first-cohort-china). The content for this program is delivered through a residential/online hybrid model. Chinese and English are both used as languages of instruction via translated online content and bilingual instructors who are located in Wuhan. The ability to translate online courses increasingly facilitates effective communication between individuals who speak different languages, and future technological innovations may allow for more interactions across language barriers.

Advances in technology, changes in personal preferences, cost factors, and even the potential impacts on cross-border mobility stemming from political action may all lead students to embrace online learning in even greater numbers over the coming decade. Partnerships can help to accelerate the expansion of these online learning programs and boost the capacity of translated curricula.

Faculty Opportunities

International partnerships can also enhance the global efforts of faculty and researchers. Across all academic fields, from art to zoology, faculty are using international partnerships to advance research and publication, artistic achievement, and other forms of scholarly work. To support these efforts, some institutions have specifically included statements about the value of global activities within their promotion and tenure policies. According to the American Council on Education's *Mapping Internationalization on U.S. Campuses: 2017 Edition* report, the percentage of U.S.-based institutions that include international work as a factor in faculty promotion and tenure decisions rose from 8 percent to 10 percent (Helms and Brajkovic 2017, 21). While modest, this represents the first increase of this data point in 10 years. There are undoubtedly faculty members on every campus engaged in some level of collaborative work across borders.

Senior administrators, and specifically senior international officers (SIOs), play a vital role as leaders of campus internationalization. However, faculty also take part in advancing and underpinning the international interests of an institution. Faculty promote education abroad to domestic students, welcome international students into their classrooms, engage in global research and publication, invite visiting scholars into their labs and offices, participate in Fulbright Programs, take their sabbaticals overseas, and help champion international efforts. Thus, when considering internationalization goals and outcomes, recognizing faculty-oriented partnerships and the contributing efforts that faculty members bring to international collaboration is critical to the success of international partnerships.

Research and Publication

Funded research partnerships serve as a prime source of international collaborations. The funding can come from multiple sources, including government funding, foundation funding, or private sector funding. Governments around the world are increasingly investing in research, with institutions within their borders serving as the prime recipients of the funding and internationally-based institutions serving as subcontractors working with the prime recipients to complete the projects. For example, a research university in New Zealand may serve as a subcontracting partner to a primary institution in Rwanda, with the funding coming from the government of Rwanda. These funded research initiatives often serve as the impetus for developing strong partnerships between the partnering institutions.

International research projects often result in joint publications with international coauthors. The Royal Society published a report titled *Knowledge,*

Networks and Nations: Global Scientific Collaboration in the 21st Century (2011), analyzing international coauthorship trends for UK scholars. Among the findings, papers that were coauthored by UK and EU scholars enjoyed higher normalized citation impact when compared with papers that were published solely by a UK author (The Royal Society 2011). Additionally, Elsevier, a global publishing conglomerate, partnered with Science Europe to better understand global authorship trends and impact (Kamalski and Plume 2013). In reviewing these trends, the authors looked at various publication categories including single author, inter-state, intra-state, and outside region (Kamalski and Plume 2013). In the case of the United States, "outside region" is defined as outside of the United States; whereas in Europe, "outside region" is defined as outside of Europe. The research shows that 30 percent of all peer-reviewed publications emanating from the United States include a coauthor outside of the United States (Kamalski and Plume 2013). Similarly, 23 percent of European publications include a non-European author (Kamalski and Plume 2013).

Collaborative publications with international coauthors can be an indicator of potential institutional partnerships. Institutions that have access to robust metrics of faculty publications should explore that information to identify the many global activities in which faculty are engaged. However, institutions should also demonstrate caution while analyzing these data. In some instances, a collaborative publication may speak more to an individual connection, and less to an institutional connection. For example, the authors of this chapter on international partnerships have worked together for many years, but their institutions do not have a formal, active partnership.

Additionally, different academic disciplines adopt varying approaches and attitudes toward scholarly publication and collaborative research. In the field of physics, for example, an article may have scores of coauthors, but the level of individual or institutional connection between any two of the authors may be minimal beyond the publication itself. Nevertheless, coauthorship can be a marker for current or potential international partnerships, particularly if two institutions exhibit a cross-disciplinary trend of coauthorship over time.

Visiting Scholars

The presence of visiting scholars on a campus can provide a guidepost to understanding the range of faculty-oriented international collaborations that could be developed into institutional partnerships. Visiting scholars typically have a short-term, temporary appointment on campus and have been invited by an individual faculty member or department. The nature of the visiting scholar's work can vary, but it often includes collaboration on a research, training, or service project. Occasionally, the visiting scholar might also "shadow" the hosting faculty member, attend courses as a guest, or observe techniques in a lab, classroom, or clinic.

It is incumbent upon the host institution to establish a welcoming environment for visiting scholars by providing adequate research and office space, access to facilities, and introductions to other scholars and students. Ideally, host institutions are also able to provide housing, ground transportation, visa support, and other services that enhance the experience of the visiting scholar, encouraging the scholar's colleagues and students to visit the campus.

Visiting scholars can share in the work of advancing international research efforts and can serve as the bridge to significant partnership activities. The visiting scholar may come from an institution that has sent many other visitors to the campus over the span of several years. In other instances, the presence of a visiting scholar might result from an alumnus or other contact who is building personal and professional connections across campuses and bringing different perspectives into labs, research facilities, classrooms, and other projects. Visiting scholars often have faculty appointments at their home institutions, or are promoted into new positions, and the relationships formed during the visiting scholars' experiences can be sustained and expanded in new ways. For all of these reasons, SIOs and partnership managers should take care to ensure that their institutional climate for visiting scholars is supportive and productive.

Other Strategic Partnership Opportunities

Global relationships can generate a range of opportunities for students and faculty, but these partnerships can also help to propel the international interests of an institution. From physical facilities to academic curricula exchanges, partnerships set into motion new activities that align strategic institutional priorities with comprehensive campus internationalization.

Academic Curricular Development and Exchanges

Higher education is a booming industry worldwide, with students from around the world increasingly demanding high-quality academic programs. In response, governments are seeking out ways to enhance the scope of their country's educational programs and increase their institutions' capacities to welcome students onto campus. To meet both demands, some governments have been contracting with higher education institutions in other countries, often in the United States, Australia, and countries in Europe, essentially to purchase and import their academic programs. For example, the Ministry of Education and Training (MOET) in Vietnam launched the Advanced Program initiative in 2005 by making a major investment to enhance higher education in the country (Nguyen and Tran 2017). MOET provided financial support to 23 Vietnamese universities in order to partner with 22 universities around the world, sharing their academic curricula from across 35 academic disciplines (Lich 2017). Thus far, more than 3,600 Vietnamese students have graduated from these programs (Lich 2017).

The Advanced Program was implemented via extensive faculty mobility. Over a multiyear period, and guided by long-term agreements, faculty from different institutions taught short courses in Vietnam, and Vietnamese faculty and visiting scholars spent considerable time at partner institutions, shadowing various academic instructors. These bilateral exchanges allowed the Vietnamese faculty members to absorb the content of the partner institutions' academic departments and eventually teach the curricula in a Vietnamese context. After some time, the curricula between the partner institutions were so well aligned that it opened the door for full student mobility between schools. In addition to the faculty mobility that was foundational in these efforts, new forms of student mobility emerged, including short-term student experiences in Vietnam and abroad, as well as collaborative academic degrees for Vietnamese students. Academic curricula exchanges, such as Vietnam's Advanced Program, help to enhance the academic engagement of student participants, bring new cultural experiences into the classrooms, and transform the work of faculty members and staff.

On a similar but smaller scale, some faculty members are invited to teach short courses at institutions around the world. The instruction can take place over an academic break or an abbreviated time during the academic year, depending on the terms of the partnership. The hosting institution usually covers the travel costs, and perhaps even remunerates the faculty member.

These teaching engagements can be personally and professionally rewarding experiences for faculty, providing them with opportunities to internationalize their course content; develop new connections that result in funded research, publications, or service; or perhaps even be presented with a joint appointment. Short-term teaching opportunities can serve to build and enrich a connection between a faculty member and an international partner.

Overseas Operations

The establishment of physical facilities in other countries to aid in-country activities like study abroad, research, and recruiting has become increasingly common for institutions worldwide. These facilities can include teaching centers, research facilities, recruiting offices, and other representative offices. In some instances, institutions establish these facilities through rental or ownership arrangements in the private marketplace. However, in other cases, partnerships play a central role in securing these facilities because the spaces are located directly on the campus of an international partner. The tax and legal implications of either owning or renting property can be particularly challenging in the international marketplace. As a result, utilizing space on the campus of an international partner can be a cost-effective and less onerous way to establish a physical presence in another country. For example, in 2015, Kobe University, a leading Japanese national university, established a liaison office within the Centre for Comparative Studies of Civilisations at the Jagiellonian University in Kraków, Poland (for more information, visit www.office.kobe-u.ac.jp/ipiep/poland/about_en.html). The on-campus office provides the space for Kobe University representatives to share information about the university with Jagiellonian students and identify other pathways for collaboration and engagement.

For faculty, this sustained presence in another country enhances their ability to engage in collaborative research with partners. Staff members who are responsible for international recruiting can also work from these international offices, thereby reducing overseas travel costs and increasing the in-country visibility of the institution. The ability to have representatives of an institution physically sitting alongside those of an international partner can strengthen the bonds of the partnership for the long term.

Some institutions are also developing large branch campuses globally, instead of bringing international students to the home campus. According to the Cross-Border Education Research Team (C-BERT), an international branch campus is "An entity that is owned, at least in part, by a foreign higher education provider; operated in the name of the foreign education provider; and provides an entire academic program, substantially on site, leading to a degree awarded by the foreign education provider" (C-BERT 2017). An institution establishes a branch campus to provide a place for international students to study from that institution's faculty and earn a degree from that institution, without requiring the students to leave their home country. International students incur reduced travel and living expenses and gain the ability to remain in their culture and stay closer to home.

A November 2016 report released jointly by the Observatory on Borderless Higher Education (OBHE) and C-BERT identified 249 international branch campuses worldwide, serving more than 180,000 students (Garrett et al. 2016). Sixty-six of those campuses were established during the five-year period leading up to the report, with China now serving as the largest host to branch campuses and the United States as the largest provider (Garrett et al. 2016).

Occasionally, branch campuses are colocated with other institutions to create a dynamic educational community, such as Qatar's Education City, which includes campuses from Carnegie Mellon, Cornell, Georgetown University, Texas A&M, and Virginia Commonwealth University (for more information, visit www.qf.org.qa/education/education-city). In other instances, the branch campus may exist alongside a partner campus, thus providing new opportunities for academic collaboration between the partner institutions. For example, Tsinghua University, in partnership with the University of Washington, recently launched the Global Innovation Exchange (GIX) (UW News staff 2015). The partnership includes a collaborative instructional facility near Seattle, Washington, and is designed to bring together students, faculty, professionals, and entrepreneurs from around the world to collaborate on technology and design projects (for more information, visit gixnetwork.org/about/places). This is the first time that a Chinese research university has established a physical presence in the United States (UW News staff 2015).

Branch campuses can address a number of institutional strategic goals, including a desire to enhance a global brand or offer an attractive destination for domestic students to engage in overseas study. On the other hand, building and operating an entire campus in another country can be quite costly for institutions. An effective partnership agreement can help to align the branch campus with the home institution's curricula, mission, and internationalization goals while also limiting in-country overhead and compliance requirements.

The Development of Partnerships

The prevalence of partnerships is on the rise, however, before new partnerships are built or expanded, institutions should survey the campus for partnership history and stakeholder interest. One way to begin this process is to develop a comprehensive inventory of the institution's existing international partnerships, which likely will involve multiple offices and schools. International offices are valuable reference points and can often provide information on partnerships that support outbound student mobility and inbound visiting students and scholars. The research office typically has access to information on research and scholarship that is either taking place in a global setting or is supported by funding from another country. The faculty affairs department often records sabbaticals and travel taken by faculty members. Institutional faculty activity reporting can serve as another source for information about faculty connections globally. A current and comprehensive inventory should be generated, detailing the status of all international partnerships that the institution has implemented, as well as denoting whether these are dormant or current, formal or informal, and ceremonial or active.

Having an inventory makes it easier to understand patterns, recognize gaps, and begin to pursue new opportunities more strategically. Because higher education institutions often operate in a decentralized manner, it is possible that several groups on a campus may be working with the same partner institution without even realizing it. If the inventory reveals a significant amount of activity with one international partner or one country or region, that may lead to more robust discussions about new opportunities with that partner or within that area.

A campuswide dialogue featuring a range of faculty and staff who already work in particular regions may produce some interesting insights. Inviting students' viewpoints, from international students and education abroad participants, can offer additional perspectives to the opportunities that are available to an institution. These information exchanges can create new interdisciplinary programs, expand research-oriented activities, increase pathways for student participation, and produce many other viable outcomes.

The programmatic expansion and diversification of existing partnerships can yield a number of benefits for an institution. First, partnerships that involve multiple layers of activities, or multiple academic disciplines, often stand a better chance of being sustainable compared with partnerships that are focused solely on one activity or one key individual. For example, if the point person leaves the institution, the partnership is at greater risk of coming to an end or becoming something that is far different from what was originally intended. On the other hand, robust partnerships that comprise multiple forms of activity, multiple people, and even multiple departments are able to more effectively weather the staff departures and programmatic adjustments. For this reason, institutions of higher education appear to be moving away from a focus on the quantity of agreements signed to the actual productivity of the partnerships. Institutions are also seeking to invest their resources into "key strategic partners" that are more likely to generate outcomes linked to student learning and faculty scholarship. Engaging in an institution-wide assessment on the status of partnerships may reveal an existing community of key strategic partners on a campus.

However, if the inventory process reveals programmatic or regional gaps, and there is a desire to launch new partnership efforts, it can be helpful to start with modest and achievable activities. Faculty exchanges, visiting scholars, and other forms of scholarly collaboration are productive ways to initiate a partnership. These types of programs can be relatively inexpensive and simple to implement, and they allow institutions to develop a level of familiarity and trust with one another. Once these faculty connections are established and active, other forms of partnership that support student mobility and academic collaboration can develop more naturally, based on a foundation built from faculty familiarity.

Whether the partnership is connected to student learning or faculty scholarship, it is prudent for a new partnership to be directly aligned with the strategic goals of the institution. A review of other institutions' websites and peer research can offer information and ideas on viable partnership activities. The partnership should also be linked to the faculty, students, or other stakeholders who will most likely be participating in the relationship and benefiting from its outcomes. Unsolicited partnerships from unknown institutions that have no relation to the home institution's mission, values, or members are often nonstarters. Whichever path an institution follows, beginning with small and tangible outcomes and seeking opportunities to build new layers can result in more productive, long-term partnerships.

Conclusion

International partnerships have increasingly become strategic priorities for institutions worldwide. They are valuable tools that allow institutions to extend new opportunities to their students, staff, and faculty in preparation for active engagement in a globalized marketplace. However, the success of these partnerships depends upon institutions having a clear understanding of what they want to achieve, recognizing the various partnership dynamics that are present, and considering the full range of activity types that are available to support campus internationalization goals. Resource-based partnerships, support-based partnerships, and complementary partnerships embody different attributes that will either facilitate or impede an institution's ability to develop collaborations that support student learning, international student enrollment, faculty engagement, and other strategic opportunities. Additionally, investing in internal mechanisms to canvass the full array of existing partnerships, and then using that information to recognize gaps or establish multidimensional strategic partnerships, can serve as a useful foundation for establishing successful and sustainable international partnerships.

References

Cross-Border Education Research Team (C-BERT). 2017. "Branch Campus Listing." Albany, NY: Cross-Border Education Research Team. http://cbert. org/resources-data/branch-campus.

Garrett, Richard, Kevin Kinser, Jason E. Lane, and Rachael Merola. 2016. *International Branch Campuses - Trends and Developments 2016.* Observatory on Borderless Higher Education and Cross-Border Education Research Team (C-BERT) at the State University of New York at Albany and Pennsylvania State University. http://www.obhe.ac.uk/documents/view_details?id=1035.

Helms, Robin Matross, and Lucia Brajkovic. 2017. *Mapping Internationalization on U.S. Campuses: 2017 Edition.* Washington, DC: American Council on Education. https://www.acenet.edu/Documents/Mapping-Internationalization-2017.pdf.

Kamalski, Judith, and Andrew Plume. 2013. *Comparative Benchmarking of European and US Research Collaboration and Researcher Mobility.* Science Europe and Elsevier's SciVal Analytics. https://www.elsevier.com/research-intelligence/research-initiatives/science-europe.

Knight, Jane. 2011. "Doubts and Dilemmas With Double Degree Programs." In "Globalisation and Internationalisation of Higher Education" [online monograph]. *Revista de Universidad y Sociedad del Conocimiento (RUSC)* 8, 2:297–312.

Knight, Jane, and Jack Lee. 2012. "International Joint, Double, and Consecutive Degree Programs: New Developments, Issues, and Challenges." In *The SAGE Handbook of International Higher Education,* eds. Darla K. Deardorff, Hans de Wit, John D. Heyl, and Tony Adams. Thousand Oaks, CA: Sage Publications.

Lich, Thanh. 2017. "Education Ministry Plans to Expand Advanced Training Program." *VietNamNet.* February 20, 2017. http://english.vietnamnet.vn/fms/

education/172778/education-ministry-plans-to-expand-advanced-training-program.html.

Nguyen, Nhai, and Ly Thi Tran. 2017. "Looking Inward or Outward? Vietnam Higher Education at the Superhighway of Globalization: Culture, Values and Changes." *Journal of Asian Public Policy* 11, 2:28–45. https://www.tandfonline.com/eprint/5xdcwWTkfT338UnevEy6/full.

The Royal Society. 2011. *Knowledge, Networks and Nations: Global Scientific Collaboration in the 21st Century.* London, United Kingdom: The Royal Society. https://royalsociety.org/~/media/Royal_Society_Content/policy/publications/2011/4294976134.pdf.

Schupp, Eugene W., Pedro Jordano, and José María Gómez. 2017. "A General Framework for Effectiveness Concepts in Mutualisms." *Ecology Letters* 20, 5:577–580.

UW News staff. 2015. "UW and Tsinghua University Create Groundbreaking Partnership with Launch of the Global Innovation Exchange." *UW News.* Seattle, WA: University of Washington. June 18, 2015. http://www.washington.edu/news/2015/06/18/uw-and-tsinghua-university-create-groundbreaking-partnership-with-launch-of-the-global-innovation-exchange.

2

Educational Mobility Partnerships

Kalpen Trivedi

The connection between travel and learning has been well established. International educational mobility can enhance students' academic or technical preparedness by enabling them to make connections across cultures, navigate difference, and operate among varied perspectives. Arguably, the world is an increasingly smaller place, and important tensions persist between the forces of globalization and national interests. Nonetheless, higher education institutions are keenly focused on preparing their graduates to compete on the global stage. Thus, increasing the avenues for both greater student mobility as well as opportunities for internationalization at home forms an important part of institutional and, indeed, national strategies. This chapter presents an overview of models of educational mobility, offers strategies for leveraging partnerships for strong education abroad programming, and looks beyond to newer models of collaborative degree program delivery.

Historical Context

Partnerships, in this context, are a relatively recent phenomena that have grown out of a desire to facilitate and provide structure to mobility activity that has been going on for a long time. Indeed, the specific connection between travel and learning is one seen from early times. In the seventh century, the Chinese Buddhist monk Hiuen Tsang (Xuanzang) spent nearly 17 years traveling through central Asia and northern India, including 2 years at the ancient university of Nalanda (in the modern day Indian state of Bihar). His *Great Tang Records on the Western Regions* serves as the primary source for the study of medieval Asia. In the High Middle Ages, from the eleventh to thirteenth centuries, student travel between the burgeoning European universities was common; for instance, an early recorded international student at Oxford University is one Emo of Friesland in 1190.

European Tradition

While that was the case in the Middle Ages, since then, many barriers to recognition have been erected, which led to the necessity of the Bologna Process, the goal of which is to ensure that same portability of degrees that existed in early medieval universities in Europe. In the European tradition, degrees were awarded by examination, so it did not matter where one acquired the knowledge so long as the individual could be examined at the university that awarded the degree. For example, Oxford University, Cambridge University, and Trinity College Dublin have recognized each other's degrees and awarded reciprocal degrees (by incorporation) since at least the sixteenth century. While these types of arrangements were likely not construed as formal accords—nor were they ever intended expressly for student mobility—they nonetheless provide some of the genesis in both form and function that drive many of today's partnerships for educational mobility.

The origins of many current models of student mobility can be traced back to the eighteenth- and nineteenth-century tradition of the Grand Tour. Most common in the British Isles, this post-university trek through France and Italy was undertaken by the scions of wealthy northern European families with the intention of experiencing firsthand the legacies of classical antiquity and the Renaissance and, more often than not, acquiring artifacts to bring to their ancestral estates. A cynical observer might discern a similar combination of commodification and consumption of the cultural experience by many of today's student travelers. The goals of modern international academic mobility, however, were more loftily conceived and grounded in an ethos of peacebuilding as well as access, equity, and inclusion.

Fulbright and Erasmus+ Programs

The Fulbright Program in the United States and the Erasmus+ Programme of the European Union are two of the most well-known international exchange programs in modern history. In 1946, Arkansas Senator J. William Fulbright introduced legislation that would establish the Fulbright Program with the goal of promoting "international goodwill through the exchange of students in the fields of education, culture and science" (U.S. Department of State Bureau of Educational and Cultural Affairs n.d.). In the senator's own words: "There is nothing obscure about the objectives of educational exchange. Its purpose is to acquaint Americans with the world as it is and to acquaint students and scholars from many lands with America as it is – not as we wish it" (U.S. Department of State Bureau of Educational and Cultural Affairs n.d.). (For more information on the Fulbright Program, visit eca.state.gov/fulbright/about-fulbright.) Given its immediate post–World War II origins, such optimism would doubtless have seemed merited.

Likewise, the Erasmus (now Erasmus+) Programme was founded the year following the landmark Single European Act of 1986, with a core objective of promoting a European identity and greater cultural integration among students of a continent pursuing deeper political integration. Erasmus+, which celebrated its 30th anniversary in 2017 and currently operates on a budget of 14.7 billion euros, now evinces the more pragmatic goals of "growth, jobs, social equity and inclusion" and "education and training" (European Commission n.d.).

This shift in perspective is not difficult to explain. Recent research has shown a strong correlation between international educational mobility and student success outcomes; for instance, see the GLOSSARI project and IES Abroad's longitudinal survey of study abroad alumni (IES Abroad 2018). The GLOSSARI (Georgia Learning Outcomes of Students Studying Abroad Research Initiative) was a federally funded project designed to assess the outcomes of study abroad at institutions across the University System of Georgia (University of Georgia 2010). GLOSSARI yielded important positive data in terms of impact on retention, persistence, time to graduation, and graduation GPA. (For more information on GLOSSARI, visit glossari.uga.edu.) The same team of researchers has now partnered with the Institute of International Education (IIE) to refresh and enlarge this study in a new project named CASSIE (Consortium for Analysis of Student Success through International

Education) to include institutions across the United States. (For more information on CASSIE, visit www.usg.edu/cassie/quick_information.)

IES Abroad's (2018) study abroad alumni survey focused on post-graduation impact of study abroad, reporting positive figures on outcomes such as successful entrance to graduate or professional programs, time to first employment, and starting salaries. At the same time, the pressure on higher education institutions, especially publicly funded ones, to revise how they articulate their value proposition in a crowded market has also influenced how the field of international education conceives of itself as contributing to individual success metrics. More and more higher education institutions are, thus, incorporating various models of international student mobility as part of their student success strategies. Developing strong relationships based on the principles of mutuality and complementarity with institutions around the globe increasingly functions as a key component of student mobility operations across program type.

On-Campus Partnerships for Student Mobility

U.S. institutions are facing a near universal imperative to grow enrollment and increase student numbers in education abroad. This strategic priority can be attributed to a variety of factors including institutional reputation, international strategic missions or mandates, student expectations, positive student outcomes, and funding structures of international offices. Education abroad offices are, therefore, continuously looking for new strategies to meet this imperative as overall study abroad numbers are slowing down among U.S. students when compared with prerecession numbers—although there are marked increases in certain disciplines (discussed in more detail later). Additionally, education abroad offices are faced with institutional pressure to diversify their study abroad population and increase access for students from underrepresented groups, whether those are disciplinary or demographic.

The Image of Education Abroad

Education abroad, as a concept, has an image problem, and one that makes it difficult to connect with and include precisely those groups that the field wants to prioritize.

There are three elements that make up this image problem. The first is the underlying philosophy behind educational mobility, the "why" of the field. Recent research on study abroad outcomes has shown two clear trends: (a) there is real evidence for what might be considered to be pragmatic student success gains in terms of graduation rates, job placements, starting salaries, and graduate school acceptance; and (b) there is little to no evidence to suggest that the loftier ideals of global citizenship are cultivated through education abroad. Despite the trends in outcome evidence, education abroad offices continue to prioritize a message of philosophical commitment to the worthy ideals of international mobility and transformative experiences, whereas the pragmatic positive outcomes are generally relegated to on-campus marketing materials or otherwise take a back seat in terms of the field's self-presentation.

A second, possibly related element of self-presentation worth noting here is that education abroad offices often think of themselves as both separate from, and often more special than, the work of universities as a whole.

Finally, while education abroad offices are rightly very conscious of their desire to deliver quality programming, even a cursory review of websites and promotional materials from universities and international education organizations reveals a preponderance of touristic images that serve to stress the travel and personal growth elements of international programs.

The result of these three elements is that education abroad all too often projects an elitist, and possibly alienating, image of educational mobility, not unlike a "Grand Tour" redux. Is it not self-defeating to suggest, whether implicitly or explicitly, that only the small percentage of students who participate in an education abroad experience is truly getting the worth of their diploma? At a time when students and their families are concerned about educational debt and career outcomes, when university administrators and funders are placing an ever-growing emphasis on time to graduation and professional outcomes, and when the very project of globalization is being recast as a zero-sum game in national and international rhetoric, international education professionals should neither assume nor presume that the ineffable, transformative benefits of internationalization still resonate as they once did. In other words, education abroad offices need to reframe the value of their work for new, external constituencies, but also for internal constituencies (Ogden 2017).

On-Campus Partnerships as Elements of Successful Mobility Partnerships

On-campus partnerships are crucial not only for successful student mobility, but also for successful mobility partnerships. For a relationship outside the institution to be viable over time and to contribute successfully to the outcomes a campus desires for its students, buy-in from other units is vital. Educational mobility partnerships will not survive the scrutiny of campus academic, compliance, and support units if the education abroad office cannot serve as a bridge between the internal and external constituencies.

Education abroad offices often enjoy strong working relationships with student affairs and student support units on campus, sharing in the goal of supporting student success. When it comes to partnering with academic units or other administrative units, however, these relationships are not always as straightforward or harmonious, even though significant cooperation may exist with individual departments or faculty members when it comes to curricular integration or short-term programs. It is all too common to hear education abroad professionals complain about being excluded or undervalued with regard to discussions of wider campus strategy or academic planning. To be sure, education abroad *does* have something special to offer, but its value to the institution lies only in so far as it can advance the goals of the institution and its academic mission; it is not valuable as an end in itself.

Many educators feel that education abroad programming needs to reorient itself to the strategic vision and mission of the institution as a whole and its academic units, while recognizing the reality that educational mobility is one of several high-impact practices students might choose to enhance their degree. This means looking beyond mapping courses in a major to enable students to study abroad or encouraging faculty to bring groups of students overseas, but rather building a partnership with academic departments and colleges to create or source programming that fits in with their overall mission and goals, with buy-in from the academic leadership.

As an example, at the University of Massachusetts Amherst, the education abroad staff are reorienting faculty-taught programming to semester-equivalent programs designed in partnership with the deans of colleges. These programs will target the same students that the colleges wish to target and deliver similar outcomes to the colleges' own desired objectives for their undergraduates. For instance, the education abroad office, in partnership with the dean of the College of Social and Behavioral Sciences, has created customized summer programs that focus on issues of social justice, race, and violence in the Global South. Similarly, the College of Nursing, in conjunction with the goals of the department leaders, is offering semester-long opportunities for students to gain perspectives in international approaches to nursing and aging. Each of these programs is anchored locally within a partner university and supported operationally by an international education organization. The academic unit, the education abroad office, and the external partner all participated in extensive discussions and dialogue during the program design phase, which means that all parties have a real ownership stake in the success of the program. On-campus units are often more willing to invest resources and faculty time to ensure the success of the programming if they are involved in building the partnership.

Beyond developing strong partnerships with on-campus academic units, education abroad offices should actively assess their own vision and mission language as well as their self-presentation in graphic and print media. To the extent possible, these materials should mirror those of the institution at large so that efforts of the education abroad office are in the service of the institution's goals. In building partnerships with on-campus units such as careers services and institutional research, the education abroad office should prioritize research, assessment, and data gathering that can demonstrate to campus leadership the added value of educational mobility in achieving mission critical goals. By partnering with university communications and public relations units, the education abroad office can get help pushing out a message that is thematically consistent with the institution's own efforts in this area (Ogden and Trivedi 2017).

Partnership Models for Educational Mobility

International educational mobility comes in various shapes. Taxonomies and vocabulary have evolved to describe these different forms of engagement, each with its own merits and challenges. Some terms such as "student exchange" or "direct enrollment" are easily comprehended, whereas others such as "island program," "faculty-led program," and "short-term program" are often conflated or confused in usage. Generally, the student exchange is considered to be an older and more traditional form of mobility partnership—although arguably, as discussed below, the island program is of similar vintage. In contrast, short-term programs have really only been in currency for 2 decades or so. What follows is a discussion of various mobility partnership models and their respective strengths and opportunities. To be successful, institutions will need to be clear about the desired outcomes of any international mobility and then assess which form of mobility partnership will align most closely with the needs of their students and faculty and with their institutional priorities.

Exchange Partnerships

In a student exchange partnership, a number of students from one university study and live at the partner university for a semester or a year, while, simultaneously, an equal number of students from the partner university go to study at the first university. These reciprocal exchange partnerships may be between particular academic units or open to all students across partnering institutions. Typically, exchange students pay the tuition for that semester or year to their home school, even though they are enrolled at the partner school. Students participating in the exchange program are usually responsible for their own local costs, such as room and board, although many exchange partnerships will include these as well, which can help create parity between otherwise incongruous economies.

Exchange partnerships rest on the idea of reciprocity or "balance," which is to say that the number of incoming and outgoing students should be equal each year, or that the balance should, at the very least, be maintained over the life of the exchange, which is usually 3 to 5 years. When partnering universities are located in countries that lack parity in their income levels or currency strength, various strategies can and should be employed to structure a mutually beneficial exchange when the standard one-for-one model would make it difficult to sustain partnerships long term. In addition to exchanging room and board, as mentioned above, universities in high-income countries may use an "n to 1" formula to allow them to offer more generous terms to the incoming students from low-income countries to keep the relationships viable. In such cases, collecting tuition and fees from several outgoing students might enable a university in a high-income location to offer a full scholarship, including travel, to a student from a low-income country partner.

The precise terms of the student exchange are codified by both universities in a formal bilateral partnership agreement that is usually signed at the highest levels of each partner university, such as the president, chancellor, provost, rector, or vice chancellor. These partnerships confer international visibility and cachet to both institutions. As such, exchange partnerships should only be entered into with partners of similar institutional profile and reputation, where there is a reasonable expectation of student interest and course availability, and where each partner can be sure of the pastoral and student support provisions of the other institution. Even in cases where the education abroad office has considerable experience in entering into and executing such agreements, the legal counsel's office should always be part of the discussions and should have approval of the partnership agreement document.

HISTORICAL CONTEXT OF EXCHANGE PARTNERSHIPS

Exchange partnerships have been utilized by higher education institutions for many years. IIE was founded in 1919 "to catalyze educational exchange" and to serve as a "central point of contact and source of information" for U.S. as well as foreign institutions of higher education (IIE n.d.). Under IIE's auspices, the first bilateral exchange was signed in 1922 between the United States and the then Czechoslovakia as a means of enabling students from different universities to participate in the mobility. Although the interwar period saw the development of education abroad program models that would develop into the junior year abroad programs (discussed in more detail later), the traditional and predominant form of mobility partnerships in the post–World

War II era was the university-to-university student exchange. These exchanges were most often managed bilaterally, but consortium agreements involving several universities or even sub-national entities were also seen (Comp 2016; Tournès and Scott-Smith 2018). In recent years, German states such as Hessen and Baden-Württemberg have been successful at establishing and supporting consortium exchanges with U.S. states or state-systems (e.g., the Baden-Württemberg exchanges with the University of Massachusetts [UMass] and University of California [UC] systems or the Hessen-Wisconsin partnership).

State-to-State Agreements

Historically, state-to-state programs (or *Landesprogrammen*) are a distinctly German model. The most active German state is Baden-Württemberg (BW), with agreements in Massachusetts, California, Connecticut, North Carolina, and Oregon in the United States, as well as some Canadian provinces. The oldest of these is the BW-Massachusetts Exchange, which has existed in some form since 1964. These exchanges are supported by the individual German state's Ministry of Science, Research and the Arts and, in the case of BW, enhanced through generous scholarship funding for both incoming and outgoing students on the exchange program through the Baden-Württemberg Stipendium.

The BW Ministry for Science, Research and the Arts also has a partnership with NAFSA: Association of International Educators and American Association of Collegiate Registrars and Admissions Officers (AACRAO) through which they offer an annual, weeklong seminar for international office staff, with all expenses in Germany funded by the BW Ministry. During the seminar, participants learn more about the educational system and institutions in BW, German-U.S. academic equivalencies, and student exchange between Germany and the United States.

BENEFITS OF EXCHANGE PARTNERSHIPS

Proponents of the exchange partnership cite the opportunity for students' full immersion in a foreign university as its chief advantage. Because the exchange partnership requires that the students become, for all intents and purposes, temporary students at the host institution with relatively little scaffolding or special treatment, this model allows for greater integration of the exchange students into the host institution's campus life. Students must familiarize themselves with the processes and administrative offices of the host institution, seek pastoral care, and often make living arrangements on the same terms as matriculated students.

Furthermore, the duration of these programs (usually a semester, but often a year) provides exchange students with the chance to engage with local students in and outside of class, thereby enriching the experience for all. Exchange students help to diversify the population of the home campus by bringing a variety of short-term nondegree students from the overseas partner institution. Even U.S. universities with aggressive international recruitment strategies for foreign students find that the majority of such students may come from a few, select countries. A strategic array of exchange partnerships can help internationalization at home by diversifying the voices and experiences represented on the U.S. campus.

Exchange programs can be relatively affordable and accessible to students because they generally pay no more than the home campus tuition and fees and they have the freedom and flexibility to economize their local expenses. Additionally, most U.S. universities allow students to use their financial aid when studying on established university exchanges. Exchange programs can, thus, provide students with the opportunity to gain international experience and cross-cultural skill sets in an economical manner.

CHALLENGES OF EXCHANGE PARTNERSHIPS

From the institutional perspective, maintaining balance is often a primary challenge of this model. The theoretical financial swap that is presumed by the exchange of a similar number of students between partner institutions can have a real financial impact if one partner cannot recruit enough students to reciprocate the other's interest. Exchange agreements are generally written so as to allow the partner institutions to decide on the precise number of students exchanged in advance of each academic year. Although institutions may tolerate minor deviations from that determined number from time to time, in the interests of sustaining the relationship, it is good practice to ensure that parity is achieved over the term of the agreement and that the count is reset at the time of any renewal or renegotiation of the exchange partnership. Partners may also be able to incorporate other models of mobility (e.g., summer schools or a customized short-term cohort) into the exchange arithmetic to ensure that mobility continues and balance is maintained.

Another challenge for many universities, especially in the United States, is the pressure to uphold specific standards of risk management and student health and safety, often as a result of state/provincial or federal requirements, within a challenging global environment. In some cases, the different types of support at partner universities may be perceived as a negative feature of such partnerships by risk-averse institutions.

Finally, it bears repeating that the success of the exchange partnership requires buy-in from every level of the university, from senior leadership and academic units to administrative offices responsible for accommodations, student records, enrollment, financial aid, and student affairs. Lack of expertise, goodwill, or capacity in any part of the university can negatively affect the exchange students' experiences, which in turn can have a deleterious effect on the partnership and, potentially, the reputation of the institution.

From the student perspective, some of the advantages discussed above are also the shortcomings of this type of mobility partnership. While the exchange program works well for the intrepid student, especially one with prior travel experience, it can be challenging for a first-generation student or a first-time traveler to confront a new academic system in an unfamiliar culture without the transitional support that many U.S. campuses typically provide.

Nontraditional students (e.g., working, part-time, family breadwinner, parent) and students who do not have a high degree of flexibility in their programs of study may find that the exchange program does not fit their needs. For example, a student who is also working part time may not be able to spend a whole semester or year away from home.

Additionally, a student may not be able to participate in the exchange program if the partner institution does not have the precise courses needed to stay on track with the home university's curriculum or graduation requirements—unless both universities are willing to invest significant time and effort in building a strong partnership where curricula align in specific degree programs. Even where the curricula match, in certain academic systems, the courses being offered in any given term are usually not decided until the start of the academic period. That uncertainly makes the exchange partnership a less viable choice for students who are in a highly sequential major or on a strict timetable to graduation. However, these challenges can also present opportunities for partnering institutions to develop their relationships further, because careful presentation of the barriers to entry and participation can sometimes lead to modifications in practice at the host institution, particularly if there is commitment across the organization.

OUTLOOK OF EXCHANGE PARTNERSHIPS

Despite exchange partnerships being the mainstay of U.S. student mobility for much of the latter half of the twentieth century, education abroad offices across the United States are finding it increasingly difficult to sustain these relationships. In addition to the risk management concerns already noted, this decline can be attributed primarily to three reasons.

First, there has been a general decline in U.S. student enrollment in programs in the liberal arts, which is where a number of such exchange partnerships originated. Concomitant with this shift is the second reason, which is the increase in enrollment in science, technology, engineering, and mathematics (STEM) and business studies and the subsequent growth of mostly short-term education abroad programming targeting these students with their more prescribed and rigid curricular requirements. In the last 3 years for which data are available, STEM programming has seen a year-on-year growth of 8 to 9 percent (IIE 2015, 2016, 2017). In 2015–16, only 7.4 percent of education abroad students were enrolled in languages and international studies compared with STEM and business studies, which saw enrollments of 25.2 percent and 20.9 percent, respectively (IIE 2017).

And finally, there has been a significant decline in language studies enrollment numbers on many college campuses across the United States. According to the Modern Language Association, enrollment "fell 9.2% between fall 2013 and fall 2016, suffering the second-largest decline in the history of the census" (Looney and Lusin 2018, 2). In consequence, students are largely choosing programs abroad that are delivered in English, with minimal foreign language study. Although an increasing number of foreign universities offer classes and degree programs in English, exchange programs cannot always guarantee the regular availability of such offerings.

None of this is to suggest that exchange partnerships are inevitably doomed. If nothing else, establishing robust relationships between strong, complementary institutions overseas undoubtedly redounds to the benefit of the universities entering into the partnership. Sustaining such partnerships, however,

---

Tips and Good Practices for Student Exchange Partnerships

TIPS

- Ensure institutional complementarity, e.g., similar student profile, complementary or similar research profile/output, similar support structures.
- Ensure mutual interest:
  - Student interest;
  - Course availability/access; and
  - Pastoral care and student services.
- Develop a mechanism to ensure that economic parity and access for participants are in place.
- Verify that the agreement specifies the terms of the exchange enacted:
  - Numbers of students per academic term or year;
  - Institutional scope of the exchange, e.g., whole institution or limited to specific departments or schools;
  - Duration of agreement/expiration of exchange relationship and terms for renewal;
  - Specific institutional responsibilities;
  - Students' responsibilities;
  - Terms for student application and acceptance, e.g., baseline GPA, language requirements, disciplinary record; and
  - Terms and means for balancing the exchange.

GOOD PRACTICES

- Ensure buy-in and support across the institution, from senior leadership (in principle) to support staff (in practice) *before* the exchange is formalized.
- Achieve parity in student numbers over the duration of the exchange.
  - Explore short-term program exchanges as a means to balance unbalanced relationships.
- Reset any balances when renewing agreements.

Work internally across the institution to build and expand exchange relationships with key partners, such as through the research affairs office.

can be challenging if they are limited solely to student mobility. Exchange partnerships have great potential to be leveraged for strategic institutional partnerships by overlaying other activities such as research collaborations and faculty exchange.

Given the institutional buy-in required to establish such relationships, the education abroad office should work with the senior international officer (SIO) as well as the office of research affairs to examine the potential for a multilayer strategic partnership when establishing, reviewing, or renewing an exchange partnership. This means taking into account faculty research interests and international expertise, auditing coauthored publications, and seeking regular input from the research affairs office, in addition to reviewing course offerings and logistical details, which are traditionally the purview of the education abroad office. If student mobility is viewed as one of the *many* activities within a strategic partnership, there is every reason for an exchange relationship to thrive.

Direct Enrollment Partnerships

The direct enrollment partnership may be viewed, for simplicity's sake, as a one-sided exchange. Under this model, the sending university establishes a relationship with the receiving university without any commitment from the latter to reciprocate. Direct enrollment does not necessitate a signed agreement between the two universities, but it is good practice to have a written agreement that stipulates the expectations and responsibilities of the two institutions to ensure duty of care to the students and to mitigate institutional liability, especially if direct billing arrangements are involved.

A written agreement can help to clarify practices and processes around questions such as how students will be billed, what kind of host university infrastructure will be available to support students, and how critical incidents will be responded to and reported, among other queries. Another benefit of establishing a formal partnership is that a tuition discount can often be negotiated, making the mobility opportunity more financially accessible to students. It should be noted that many private institutions in the United States employ a home school tuition model, under which the outbound student incurs habitual charges regardless of the actual costs of the international experience. Equally, though, such institutions often create bespoke inbound programs and pricing structures for direct-enroll students from partner institutions.

BENEFITS OF DIRECT ENROLLMENT PARTNERSHIPS

Direct enrollment partnerships offer many of the same advantages as exchange partnerships, such as the opportunity for students' immersion and integration into campus life. Direct enrollment partnerships, however, can often be easier to sustain because there are no issues about balancing student numbers. As long as there is sufficient interest in the partner university and good availability of relevant coursework, it is easy to maintain mobility.

Many universities, most notably in Australia, Ireland, New Zealand, and the United Kingdom, offer such partnership opportunities, which are often referred to as "study abroad" options. As universities in these countries have also traditionally been favored by many institutions as exchange partners, engaging the direct enrollment partnership can offer a mechanism whereby temporary imbalance in the exchange partnership or a sudden surge of student interest in a particular destination can be easily accommodated. For instance, if the imbalance is such that the home institution cannot send a student through the exchange, or if there are more viable applications for spots than the exchange allows, the direct enrollment partnership will still allow the student to enroll at the partner university without a negative impact on the exchange. Moreover, in situations where it is not clear if a new exchange relationship might be sustainable (either on account of academic match or student interest), the direct enrollment model can allow an institution to test the flow of mobility with interested, fee-paying students before embarking on an exchange partnership.

CHALLENGES OF DIRECT ENROLLMENT PARTNERSHIPS

The drawbacks with regard to exchange partnerships noted above also apply to direct enrollment partnerships. Tuition models vary, with some (mainly private) institutions charging outbound participants home institution tuition and paying the direct-enroll partner on the students' behalf. Other institutions structure the relationship such that students pay tuition and fees directly to the host institutions, which may pose a financial burden on students if these fees are not comparable to the students' home institution tuition. Although, as noted above, discounts are often a feature of formally established direct enrollment partnerships.

Unlike in the case of exchange programs, in the U.S. context, many universities adopt different policies when it comes to allowing financial aid to be used for other forms of overseas study options, including direct enrollment. This measure is in place because students who leave campus without any financial obligation to the home university can represent lost tuition revenue. Many institutions may therefore elect to charge students for some portion of their usual financial dues in addition to what is payable to the host institution. Thus, in assessing direct enrollment partnerships, it is important to weigh the capacity created for student mobility against institutional fee structures and to consider whether the cost will be a deterrent to access to studying abroad. Nonetheless, in the strategic design of the direct enrollment partnership, it may be possible to create specific curricular pathways to build opportunities and capacity in areas where a university-wide exchange agreement may not be viable.

> **Good Practices for Direct Enrollment Partnerships**
>
> • Utilize direct enrollment partnerships when there is disparity between student supply and the desire from partnering institutions to engage institutionally.
>
> • Commit terms for enrollment and financial obligations to paper, i.e., formalize an agreement.
>
> • Explore various financial models and ensure that cost is not a deterrent to participation.

Island Programs

There are other modern models of educational mobility, often conflated in the term "island programs," that should be considered for potential partnerships, including junior year abroad programs, faculty-led or faculty-taught short-term programs (often referred to as "custom programs"), and study centers. They all originate in activities of the home campus, and there can be considerable overlap of goals and organizational elements among the programs. It is important to note that while "island program" has pejorative connotations, it is a commonly used phrase within U.S. education abroad. (For an overview of island programs, see Hanouille and Leuner 2001; Hernandez, Wiedenhoeft, and Wick 2014.)

JUNIOR YEAR ABROAD PROGRAMS

Formal junior year abroad (JYA) programs are more often available in the liberal arts and usually, although not exclusively, at private U.S. institutions. The mechanism for student mobility is generally established as an institutional direct enrollment partnership with a regular flow of students from particular departments on the home campus that have integrated the year overseas at the partner institution into the course of study pursued at the home institution. Students on JYA programs are received by the host institutions as they would any exchange or direct enrollment students—although many U.S. institutions will broker some customized arrangements with the foreign university or scaffold the JYA with their own support services or faculty. These arrangements may include home or host university faculty/staff serving as "resident directors" with pastoral responsibility for the students, specialized curriculum, or cultural and cocurricular programming or excursions arranged for the visiting student cohort.

The University of Delaware (UD) can claim the distinction of the first "education abroad" (island) program in the United States, dating back to 1923 when a group of eight students went to France for a six-week program, which became the basis for UD's Junior Year Abroad Program (UD 2016). A similar program was introduced at Smith College in 1926 with a group going to Paris, followed by the establishment of a program in Florence in 1931, the first U.S. university with a formal presence in Florence (Comp 2016; Smith College n.d.). Such programs were often the result of the passion and dedication of individual faculty members who, with varying degrees of buy-in and assistance from the home institution, would be responsible for arranging the program of study, managing the logistics, and accompanying the student groups, whether the program lasted for short durations or entire semesters. Indeed, it was not unusual, even for early exchange programs, to have key faculty members serve as residential directors in the host city, thereby providing a home campus connection for the student cohort overseas. For several years after the program's inception in 1964, the University of Massachusetts Amherst's English Department would send a faculty member with students on the exchange program with the University of Freiburg in Germany. The program was eventually incorporated into the state-to-state exchange agreement between the UMass system and Baden-Württemberg, evidencing the generative development that educational mobility partnerships can undergo.

SHORT-TERM FACULTY-LED PROGRAMS

Short-term faculty-led programs have been steadily on the rise, especially in the last 2 decades. Across the United States, between the academic years 2005–06 and 2015–16, participation in summer term education abroad programming hovered around 38 percent, while enrollment in programs of 8 weeks or less during the academic year grew from 9.5 to 17.4 percent (IIE 2017). As noted above in the discussion of exchange partnerships, at the same time that enrollment in the traditional liberal arts disciplines has declined in the United States, education abroad programming has been responding to the desire from STEM and business studies students for international mobility opportunities. The lock-step sequence of many STEM degrees, and the increasing stress on business students completing co-ops and internships, often means that students in those disciplines cannot spend a full semester or year overseas without increasing their time to degree completion.

As a result, topically organized short-term programs that are taught by faculty from the home campus have become a popular way for many institutions to offer these students an education abroad experience. Given the widespread desire to grow numbers in education abroad, these programs, often entrepreneurial in nature and relying heavily on charismatic faculty members for their success, present an attractive strategy for many institutions to grow education abroad enrollment and get faculty buy-in, especially within academic units without a strong tradition of education abroad activity.

Short-term and faculty-led programs can often successfully engage partnerships with higher education institutions abroad, as well as with international education organizations (discussed in more detail later). Partnering with universities abroad to develop such programs is a good way of not only extending the institution's educational capacity by engaging with complementary or supplementary expertise in the host country, but also building in opportunities for interaction with local communities and students. In developing such programs, universities are often responding to both student demand and distinct national strategies and funding opportunities aimed at increasing the numbers of students moving between countries, with competitions such as those under the 100,000 Strong in the Americas from the U.S. Department of State, the Transatlantic Mobility Program with France, and the New Colombo Plan in Australia.

STUDY CENTERS

A number of well-resourced universities with large education abroad programs have established study centers or campuses overseas to deliver their own education abroad programming in strategically chosen locations. Although the majority of these study centers and foreign campuses are usually established by private institutions, there are notable examples from public universities as well. Examples of study centers include the New York University Global Academic Centers, the Monash University Prato Centre, the Brigham Young University Jerusalem Center, and the Stanford Bing Overseas Studies Program centers, as well as the University of Georgia's centers at Oxford, England; Cortona, Italy; and San Luis de Monteverde, Costa Rica, to name a few.

These international study centers undertake a gamut of activities, from coordinating education abroad activities or overseas housing to enrolling local students from the foreign location into programs offered by the home institution. In the case of study centers used primarily for educational mobility, institutions often still find it useful to establish partnerships with local foreign universities to deliver instruction, engage local faculty and students, and offer access to student clubs and other integrative experiences. It may be argued that the extent to which such a center-based program is successful depends in large part on the strength of the partnership established by the home institution and the local academic community and area organizations.

An institution seeking to engage in the study center model would do well to begin by choosing an academic partner institution that aligns strategically with its own needs and priorities, is of similar academic reputation, and has the political capital to facilitate the home institution's transition into the overseas space. As with short-term programs, a strong partnership with a local, high-quality academic institution can extend the home campus's capacity to deliver varied educational programming, as well as bring contextual, logistical, and risk management expertise to enable the home institution to deliver its programs successfully in a foreign location.

BENEFITS OF ISLAND PROGRAMS

These models of student mobility are centered on the home campus, which presents several advantages to both the institution and its students. First, control of the academic programming means that institutions can ensure that their students are getting the courses and credits they need overseas and are able to count these toward their degree requirements seamlessly. Education abroad offices can work from the ground up with academic units on the home campus to integrate these overseas opportunities into the curriculum at home. Universities are also able to verify that the programs' academic standards are equivalent to those on the home campus. For the students, there is very little uncertainty about both the coursework and the administrative process, and they can be guided by home university staff through any related issues encountered on the program.

Second, these island program models present a risk management advantage. To the extent that the home institution is running its own centers and programs overseas or delivering tailored educational programming in partnership with local universities, it is much easier for the home university to exercise oversight over risk management and student health and safety issues. The home institution can continue to administer its code of conduct and policies, for instance, and provide uninterrupted access to home campus support services while the students are abroad.

The partnership with the local academic institution can offer additional support by providing students with access to locally relevant support structures, as well as help with navigating any legal or security situations. In locations where the security or political situation may be sensitive, a partnership with a local university can be invaluable for risk mitigation and crisis response. A good partnership agreement will stipulate the expectations and responsibilities for both parties and, to the extent possible under local law, enable the home institution to comply with home country regulations, such as Title IX and the Clery Act in the United States. Students and their families often find the presence of the home institution reassuring, especially in the case of inexperienced travelers.

Third, island programs can be a good way to encourage underrepresented student populations to study abroad because they would continue to have access to the support structures and communities from their home campus. Any scholarships or special financial access arrangements that students may have on their home campus can be easily replicated in the partnerships. Such funding support and transferability often depends on institutional philosophy vis-à-vis academic mobility structures and institutional risk tolerance. For instance, some institutions make no distinction between study abroad opportunities and allow broad portability of all financial aid and scholarships; others allow funding to only be applied to university "owned," directed, or managed programming.

Additionally, island programs, especially when delivered in partnership with a local university, have the potential to evolve into larger generative relationships. The regular flow of students and faculty can lead to opportunities for graduate placement and research collaborations, which in turn enhance the reputations of both universities. If the partnership is a good strategic and curricular fit, other models of educational mobility, including the joint delivery of degrees (discussed in more detail later), can also result from this model. As the partnership matures, it has the potential to involve the wider communities through sister-city and sister-state relationships, thus enhancing the civic stature of both institutions.

CHALLENGES OF ISLAND PROGRAMS

These models of student mobility are open to common criticisms. First, the fact that students from the home campus travel in cohorts, often to destinations and universities where there is already a high concentration of U.S.

students, can be a deterrent to their integration and engagement with local students, the host university, and the culture. The island nature of these programs means that the U.S. students may not have to encounter or navigate the challenging situations in which true cross- and inter-cultural development can occur, unless the programs are intentionally designed to facilitate such growth and interaction.

Research shows that the measurable impact in terms of linguistic ability and global mindedness is perceptibly higher among students who participate in longer-term or non-island programs (Dwyer 2004; Kehl and Morris 2007; Medina-Lopez-Portillo 2004). Arguably, this lack of cross-cultural development may not be a shortcoming of the length or nature of island programs themselves, but rather a misalignment of a particular program's design and desired outcomes. As noted above, a strong partnership with a local academic institution can mitigate this insular effect by providing opportunities for purposeful engagement and interaction with domestic students and the local community. In the absence of such an underlying academic partnership, the island program will need to plan intentionally to structure such opportunities into the program design.

Another potential challenge of many of these programs is that they often rely heavily on the same faculty member or group of faculty members year after year. Undoubtedly, the programs thrive on the commitment of these faculty members, but if a sense of ownership of the programs and the attendant partner relationships abroad becomes entrenched, it can become difficult for the education abroad office to make much needed structural changes to the programs or introduce modifications to align with best practices in the field. Moreover, in such cases, the retirement or departure of the faculty member(s) could sound the death knell of the program.

Ideally, these programs should be run as a true collaboration between the education abroad office, the faculty member(s), and their departments. It is also important that institutions empower the education abroad office appropriately to review and oversee the logistical, financial, and health and safety management of island programs, or they can come to pose a high degree of liability to the institution. When island programs are also associated with an overseas center (i.e., the home institution is also responsible for managing a physical infrastructure overseas), these issues of liability and risk management can often greatly multiply in scope. In these cases, the home institution may have to consider local labor laws and reporting or oversight in fiscal or property management matters in addition to any home country/campus obligations. A strong partnership with an in-country higher education institution may be a good solution to supplement the education abroad office's knowledge base and capacity to manage such a center, while also providing the richer engagement opportunities for students as noted above.

Lastly, funding and financing for these island programs can vary widely depending on institutional practices. If students are able to access these programs at costs equivalent to the cost of attendance at their home school and can carry their financial aid with them, such programs can be a strong strategy for enrollment growth and access. Ideally, the financial design of the program will incorporate mechanisms such as permitting faculty to teach on-load and allowing the program budget to access tuition dollars, among others, which can help to contain the costs of island programs. If, however, these programs are seen as merely revenue mechanisms for the home campus and they add additional financial burden to the students, then they will serve to corroborate the misperception that education abroad opportunities are available only to an elite group of students. This is especially true for low-credit short-term summer programs because U.S. federal financial aid can only be applied to summer enrollment of six credits or higher and, even then, most of the aid is in the form of unsubsidized loans.

It may be possible, for some universities, to leverage existing exchange or direct enrollment partnerships to create capacity and control costs on short-term programs under certain circumstances. For instance, a short-term or faculty-taught component could be customized as part of an existing summer school at an overseas university, which would allow both partners to benefit from economies of scale, or even creatively balance exchanges that tilt unfavorably in one direction. As these last few observations note, the many advantages of island programs could be greatly enhanced through the strategic cultivation or inclusion of other types of mobility partnerships.

Other Forms of Mobility

The models of mobility discussed above represent the primary mechanisms for U.S. undergraduate student mobility as part of their degree programs. Beyond these, there are other emergent modes of student mobility that can offer students additional sustained international experiences, strengthen an institution's international and research profiles, and serve as a mechanism for increasing or managing enrollment.

COLLABORATIVE DEGREE MODEL

An important mode of student mobility that is gaining attention and popularity is through the "collaborative degree" model. The landscape of such partnerships is littered with often conflated and confusing terminology, and terms such as "joint degree," "dual degree," "double degree," and "sequential degree" are often heard. In the report *Mapping International Joint and Dual Degrees: U.S. Program Profiles and Perspectives*, the American Council on Education (ACE) defines two principal types: the "joint degree" is a "program that is designed and delivered by two or more partner institutions in different countries [with]…a single qualification endorsed by each institution," and the "dual (or double) degree" is a "program that is designed and delivered by two or more partner institutions in different countries [with]…a qualification from each of the partner institutions" (ACE 2014, 6). The dual or double degree can come in many nuances; for example, the qualifications may be sequential or at different levels, they may be in related but different fields, or they may be the same degree.

Arguably, the recent rise in interest in such collaborative degree delivery partnerships stems from the Bologna Accord in 1999, whereby countries of the European Higher Education Area sought to streamline and align educational qualifications in member states. Following this, the European University Association (EUA) proposed a Joint Masters Project in 2002 that was intended to build on the Bologna Process as a vision of cooperation in European higher education (EUA 2004). The enthusiasm for collaborative degree provision has generally been greater in Europe, Asia, and the Pacific region, with the United States as a comparatively late entrant to the field.

The usual mechanism for such a degree centers on an articulation arrangement of the "n+n" model, whereby two institutions enter into a formal agreement to either send or receive students who have completed a certain portion of their education at one institution to finish it up at the partner institution for the receipt of previously determined credentials. For instance, a U.S. student might spend his or her final semester at a university overseas and, by virtue of the articulated, overlapping coursework, complete his or her U.S. degree program requirements. Equally, an international student may complete some years of his or her degree overseas and, through an articulation agreement, access a degree program at the U.S. partner institution.

Collaborative degree arrangements generally grow out of mutual intellectual and academic interests between partner universities. Dual degrees of various types are generally easier to set up, requiring only institutional-level approvals as they articulate the partnership between the two universities. Joint degrees are considerably more complex as they require approvals from governance boards, accrediting bodies, or even government agencies, depending on the country, because they are distinctly new degrees.

The most successful collaborative degree partnerships will be the ones that result from a deep, prior engagement between institutions. In a recent IIE survey involving 245 higher education institutions from 28 different countries, 43 percent of the institutions reported that all levels of the institution were involved in the development of such partnerships, as opposed to the 16 percent of institutions that reported a top-down approach led by administration (Obst, Kuder, and Banks 2011, 24). Studies on the best practices for developing successful collaborative partnerships are unanimous in recommending that buy-in has to exist from the highest levels of the institution down to the departments delivering the instruction and the offices responsible for administration, otherwise the partnerships will wither on the vine of the memorandum of understanding.

BENEFITS OF COLLABORATIVE DEGREES

Collaborative degrees are a form of high-impact mobility, and partnerships can ensure both some transient association for the student and a compelling and articulated choice of credential. The structure of mobility is logical and inherent to the curriculum design, and it relies not on student choice but rather the perceived value to the credential itself. The beneficial impact of international collaborative degrees is well noted for students in terms of greater training and research opportunities and the combining of cultural competencies with technical knowledge. Moreover, the efficiencies in coursework often represented by these arrangements can save students time and money in their higher education careers.

Collaborative degree partnerships also allow faculty to widen their research networks, which, in turn, enables institutions to leverage greater research capacities and build brand awareness in foreign markets (Council of Graduate Schools 2010). Indeed, beyond the obvious benefits to students and faculty, these articulated degrees may be used by universities to recruit well-qualified, high-paying international students in different markets as an enrollment management tactic and strategic budgetary enhancement. For example, a well-known university may develop a partnership with a college or education provider overseas whereby the provider delivers 'n' years of preparatory or general coursework under the control of the university. Then, upon completion of the coursework, the students may move into residence at the university to complete their degree. One such case is the Jakarta International College in Indonesia, which provides articulated pathways to U.S. and Australian universities including Western Michigan University and Monash University, respectively.

Another prominent example is the Coventry University Group, a private university in the United Kingdom, which leverages a vast range of articulated partnerships throughout the world to attract international students. The university has partners in 32 countries, including the United Kingdom (Coventry University n.d.). Such articulated degree partnerships ensure that the home institution receives well-qualified, fee-paying students, and that the students moving between locations are able to save a considerable portion on the high cost of an overseas education, especially if they hail from a low(er)-income country.

CHALLENGES OF COLLABORATIVE DEGREES

Despite the benefits observed above, it is important to note that international collaborative degree partnerships are not without their challenges. These partnerships can be time-consuming and resource-intensive to set up, complicated to govern, fraught with legal complexities, and difficult to fund and sustain over the long term (EUA 2004; Obst, Kuder, and Banks 2011). Beyond the administrative challenges, experts often note the difficulties of navigating issues related to language of instruction, the creation of new courses and curricula, inequality of access, and the consistency of academic quality control across national borders (EUA 2004; Maierhofer, Krawagna, and Kriebernegg 2010). Additionally, concerns may abound, most notably within the U.S. context, over issues such as brand dilution, double counting, and credential inflation (ACE 2014; Obst, Kuder, and Banks 2011). These and other challenges have been pivotal to the dialogues surrounding international collaborative degrees.

Undoubtedly, student mobility is an integral part of these collaborative degree models. In the 2011 IIE survey, more than 90 percent of respondents indicated that they had no interest in developing collaborative or articulated degrees that excluded student mobility (Obst, Kuder, and Banks 2011). But collaborative degrees are not a suitable partnership model for just that one purpose. These partnerships are complex to set up and manage, but when they serve to cement long-standing academic collaborations between faculty at strategically chosen partner institutions, they have tremendous potential in encouraging a virtuous circle of teaching, research, engagement, and mobility. Ultimately, these partnerships are the culmination of multifaceted and strategic relationships wherein the teaching, research, and engagement missions of the partnering universities come together.

Research Student Mobility Model

Another model of academic mobility, largely seen in the graduate arena, may be loosely termed as "research student mobility," wherein master's program or doctoral degree students spend some time at a foreign institution for research or field work for their degree. Such mobility is frequently ad hoc upon the invitation by colleagues and collaborators.

While this educational mobility model does not require a formal, written partnership agreement between the universities involved, such an agreement is often desirable. In cases where true research complementarity exists and the partnership is entered into as a strategic priority, a written agreement can serve as the basis for accessing grants from funding bodies, and it can help to reify the relationship between two laboratories, two departments, or even two universities beyond just the mutual research interest of the initiating faculty. A formal research partnership may include provisions for joint supervision of doctoral projects or cotutelles, arrangements for exchanging faculty with or without teaching provision. The agreement would codify the responsibilities and duty of care toward visiting students, which is especially relevant as the desire to provide research experiences for undergraduates continues to grow.

Additionally, a formal partnership agreement for the purposes of research mobility would protect each university's intellectual property and include safeguards for complying with U.S. export control or proprietary research regulations by ensuring that visitors to campus are appropriately vetted. If such research mobility partnerships are not within the purview of the education abroad office, those in such positions should familiarize themselves with these kinds of partnerships or opportunities on their campus. They should also consider aligning undergraduate exchange opportunities with research mobility partnerships to grow exchange mobility in a sustainable way and to strategically engage faculty champions.

International Education Organizations

While many mobility partnerships are developed between two or more colleges or universities, the post-secondary landscape is awash with organizations that provide access to education abroad opportunities for students. Within the field of education abroad, the term "provider" generally refers to a wide array of entities—not including U.S. colleges and universities—whose primary activity is to provide overseas programming. (For an overview of how "providers" operate within the U.S. study abroad arena, see Heyl 2011.) The use of external organizations or providers is most typical in the United States. These international education organizations can be consortia such as the Council on International Education Exchange (CIEE) or the University Studies Abroad Consortium (USAC); degree-providing institutions such as the School for International Training (SIT); or for-profit or not-for-profit corporate entities such as CAPA: The Global Education Network, International Studies Abroad (ISA), IES Abroad, or Academic Programs International (API).

Equally varied is the set of terms applied to designate such entities. The term "third-party provider" is laden with complexity and suggests a transactional rather than education-based relationship. Other nomenclature such as "international education provider" or "international education organization" is beginning to appear in the field, the latter being advocated by many of these organizations. A number of U.S. higher education institutions have further taken to using the term "partner organization" to acknowledge the fact that their programs have been vetted and that they share in the educational mission and duty of care for students (Kurtzman and Holloway n.d.; Ogden 2015).

Benefits of Partnering with International Education Organizations

Partnering with carefully selected international education organizations offers several benefits to institutions. The range of services provided by these partners can include facilitating direct enrollment of U.S. students at universities overseas, curating cocurricular and extracurricular activities in-country, providing customized support for short-term and faculty-led programs, and operating full-fledged study centers of their own.

These relationships can be a useful strategy for an education abroad office seeking to extend international opportunities that tie in with nontraditional study abroad disciplines, such as the STEM fields, and with professional degrees, such as nursing, because such organizations can cultivate and develop course offerings that would otherwise necessitate significant time and resource investment by the home institution. Furthermore, these partnerships allow the education abroad office to meet the demand for international options in cocurricular activities encouraged on the home campus, such as field studies, undergraduate research, internships, community engagement, and service learning. Through strategic alignment of practices and priorities, the education abroad office can use partner organizations to extend its capacity and meet goals rather than tread water in straitened financial circumstances. (For some strategies on using international education organizations to expand capacity, see Ogden 2018.)

International education organizations also offer a distinct advantage to universities in terms of risk management and student support. Because many of these organizations have widespread in-country resources, including local staff, they are able to extend the university's capacity to be responsive during a crisis, and they can offer a level of support and response to the students that would meet the home campus's expectations.

Additionally, established international education organizations, by virtue of their scale and resources, can often devote themselves to longitudinal assessments of their programs and the impact of education abroad on student outcomes, such as IES Abroad's (2018) alumni survey mentioned above. This is a value-added dimension that most education abroad offices, stretched as they are with staffing and resources, would do well to consider when looking at partnerships, especially if staff can leverage those resources for joint assessment projects.

Considerations for Partnering with International Education Organizations

Just as with any other partnership, working with international education providers requires careful consideration and an honest assessment of some concerns and possible shortcomings. Universities need to be careful in assessing the quality of the academic programming offered by such organizations, particularly in a market that is expanding all the time. The sheer number of international education organizations, and their seemingly similar programming, can make it difficult to assess quality and fit for an institution without a careful and thorough evaluation.

Even within the range of programs offered by a single provider, not all destinations and academic programs are created equal. Education abroad offices need to look deeply at the academic partners, host institutions, and faculty credentials of the various programs offered by different organizations before making their selection. For smaller offices, a good strategy might be to cultivate a close relationship with a handful of international education organizations so that staff can be well acquainted with the program offerings. Offices with greater staff and resource capacity, and thus a greater ability to assess organizations' offerings comprehensively, may be able to pick and choose programs from among a larger number of options. Moreover, although some international education organizations are able to offer varied academic programming at low costs, they are left open to the same criticisms as the island programs with regard to students' immersion levels, integration with the host community, and development of linguistic skills.

Institutions should assess their individual needs, values, and objectives thoroughly before finding the best-fit partners. As with exchange and direct enrollment partnerships, a formal, signed affiliation or consortium agreement should codify the terms of the partnership with the selected international education organization. There are often concrete benefits to entering an agreement, such as access to program familiarization visits and discounted program costs for students, but, more importantly, the partnership document can lay out the responsibilities and expectations of both parties.

Conclusion

Educational mobility is founded on relationships, and the success of the endeavor depends on the strength of the partnerships both inside and outside of the university. The international education office has a vital role to play in engaging, fostering, and sustaining partnerships that enhance students' experiences and education and support the institution's overall mission and goals.

When entering into any partnership, it is important to begin from a clear understanding and assessment of the objectives and priorities of the institution and its academic units for the education of the students, and then align mobility partnerships to serve those needs. The quality of students' experiences and outcomes is not ultimately determined by the type or duration of the model, but rather the quality of the partnership, the program design, and the capacity to deliver educational outcomes.

To this end, most higher education institutions will need to employ a judicious mix of mobility partnerships. Over time, the most successful partnerships will likely be the ones that can strategically combine various strands of activity (e.g., teaching, research, faculty engagement, and experiential learning) into multifaceted partnerships, such as a collaborative degree partnership or a long-standing research mobility partnership, which produce high impacts on the campus's international profile.

References

American Council on Education (ACE). 2014. *Mapping International Joint and Dual Degrees: U.S. Program Profiles and Perspectives.* Washington, DC: American Council on Education. http://www.acenet.edu/news-room/ Documents/Mapping-International-Joint-and-Dual-Degrees.pdf.

Comp, David. 2016. "A Historical Overview of International Education Scholarship and the Role of the Scholar-Practitioner." In *International Higher Education's Scholar-Practitioners: Bridging Research and Practice*, eds. Bernhard Streitwieser and Anthony C. Ogden. Oxford, United Kingdom: Symposium Books.

Council of Graduate Schools. 2010. *Joint Degrees, Dual Degrees, and International Research Collaborations.* Washington, DC: Council of Graduate Schools.

Coventry University. n.d. "See Our Partners Across the World." Coventry, United Kingdom: Coventry University. https://www.coventry.ac.uk/ international-students-hub/partnerships-and-places-to-study/see-our-partners-across-the-world.

Dwyer, Mary M. 2004. "More Is Better: The Impact of Study Abroad Program Duration." *Frontiers: The Interdisciplinary Journal of Study Abroad* 10:151–63. https://www.iesabroad.org/system/files/More%20is%20better%20 %28Dwyer%2C%202004%29.pdf.

European Commission. n.d. "What is Erasmus +?" European Commission. https://ec.europa.eu/programmes/erasmus-plus/about_en#tab-1-0.

European University Association (EUA). 2004. *Developing Joint Masters Programmes for Europe: Results of the EUA Joint Masters Project: March 2002– Jan 2004.* Brussels, Belgium: European University Association. https://eua.eu/resources/publications/665:developing-joint-masters-programmes-for-europe.html.

Hanouille, Leon, and Peter Leuner. 2001. "Island Programs: Myths and Realities in International Education." World Education News & Reviews (WENR). January 1, 2001. https://wenr.wes.org/2001/01/ewenr-jan-feb-2001-feature.

Hernandez, Magnolia, Margaret Wiedenhoeft, and David Wick, eds. 2014. *NAFSA's Guide to Education Abroad: For Advisers and Administrators, Fourth Edition.* Washington, DC: NAFSA: Association of International Educators.

Heyl, John D. 2011. *Third-Party Program Providers and Education Abroad: Partner or Competitor?* AIEA Occasional Papers. Durham, NC: Association of International Education Administrators. http://www.aieaworld.org/assets/docs/OccasionalPapers/third%20party%20providers-%20heyl-%20op.pdf.

IES Abroad. 2018. "Alumni Survey Results." Chicago, IL: IES Abroad. https://www.iesabroad.org/study-abroad/benefits/alumni-survey-results.

Institute of International Education (IIE). n.d. "History." Washington, DC: Institute of International Education. https://www.iie.org/en/Why-IIE/History.

Institute of International Education (IIE). 2015. *Open Doors Report on International Educational Exchange.* Washington, DC: Institute of International Education.

Institute of International Education (IIE). 2016. *Open Doors Report on International Educational Exchange.* Washington, DC: Institute of International Education.

Institute of International Education (IIE). 2017. *Open Doors Report on International Educational Exchange.* Washington, DC: Institute of International Education.

Kehl, Kevin, and Jason Morris. 2007. "Differences in Global-Mindedness Between Short-Term and Semester-Long Study Abroad Participants at Selected Private Universities." *Frontiers: The Interdisciplinary Journal of Study Abroad* 15:67–79.

Kurtzman, Rich, and Kris Holloway. n.d. "10 Quick Tips for Working with Higher Education Institutions."

Looney, Dennis, and Natalia Lusin. 2018. *Enrollments in Languages Other Than English in United States Institutions of Higher Education, Summer 2016 and Fall 2016: Preliminary Report.* New York, NY: Modern Language Association of America. https://www.mla.org/content/download/83540/2197676/2016-Enrollments-Short-Report.pdf.

Maierhofer, Roberta, Ulrike Krawagna, and Ulla Kriebernegg. 2010. *Diversifying University Studies: Joint Degrees as a New Model of Academic Mobility.*

Medina-Lopez-Portillo, Adriana. 2004. "Intercultural Learning Assessment: The Link Between Program Duration and the Development of Intercultural Sensitivity." *Frontiers: The Interdisciplinary Journal of Study Abroad*, 10:179–200.

Obst, Daniel, Matthias Kuder, and Clare Banks. 2011. *Joint and Double Degree Programs in the Global Context: Report on an International Survey.* Washington, DC: Institute of International Education.

Ogden, Anthony C. 2015. *Ten Quick Tips for Working with Education Abroad Provider Organizations*. AIEA Issue Brief. Durham, NC: Association of International Education Administrators. http://www.aieaworld.org/assets/docs/Issue_Briefs/issue%20brief-ogden.pdf.

Ogden, Anthony C. 2017. "Defending the Value Proposition of Education Abroad? Get Realistic." *International Educator* XXVI, 5:48–51.

Ogden, Anthony C. 2018. "Expanding Education Abroad Capacity Through Partnerships." *ISA Today* (blog). June 11, 2018. https://isatoday.wordpress.com/2018/06/11/ed-abroad-capacity.

Ogden, Anthony C., and Kalpen Trivedi. 2017. *The Seven Habits for Sustainable Education Abroad Growth*. AIEA Issue Brief. Durham, NC: Association of International Education Administrators. http://www.aieaworld.org/assets/docs/Issue_Briefs/ogden_trivedi_issue_brief.pdf.

Smith College. n.d. "Smith in Florence: At a Glance." Northampton, MA: Smith College. https://www.smith.edu/studyabroad/spa_florence.php.

Tournès, Ludovic, and Giles Scott-Smith, eds. 2018. *Global Exchanges: Scholarships and Transnational Circulations in the Modern World*. New York, NY: Berghahn.

University of Delaware (UD) Institute for Global Studies. 2016. "Our History." Newark, DE: University of Delaware. http://www1.udel.edu/global/studyabroad/information/brief_history.html.

University of Georgia. 2010. "Glossari: Georgia Learning Outcomes of Students Studying Abroad Research Initiative." Athens, GA: University of Georgia. http://glossari.uga.edu.

U.S. Department of State Bureau of Educational and Cultural Affairs. n.d. "About Fulbright." Washington, DC: United States Department of State Bureau of Educational and Cultural Affairs. https://eca.state.gov/fulbright/about-fulbright.

3

International Research Partnerships

Kiki Caruson

Knowledge generation knows no geographic boundaries. The grand challenges of today cannot be solved by the knowledge generated by any one nation, industry, organization, entity, or individual. Rather, collective, interdisciplinary problem-solving, which is often accomplished through partnerships, is an absolute necessity. Cooperation in the fields of science and technology accelerates economic prosperity and sustainable development across societies. Even when diplomatic relations are strained, scientific lines of communication between countries typically remain open when most other forms of contact have collapsed. For example, during the cold war, U.S. scientists maintained ties with their counterparts in the Soviet Union. Today, scholars from U.S. institutions continue to connect with their counterparts in Cuba despite restrictive policies at the national levels.

These partnering relationships are a valuable asset and promote goodwill across nations. Rather than treating competition for science and technology innovation as a "zero-sum game, U.S. scientists and institutions should sustain the free exchange of ideas and enter collaborations with strong agreements that articulate the mutual benefits for all participants and the arrangements for sharing outputs and benefits" (Colglazier and Lyons 2014). This chapter explores best practices for developing productive, sustainable, and impactful research partnerships.

Value and Need for Research and Development

Historically, the United States has been the leader globally in research and development (R&D) and technology innovation, but other nations are now devoting more and more resources to their R&D efforts. According to the *2017 Global R&D Funding Forecast*, "until 2007, the Americas [North and South] dominated total R&D spending, now it is the Asian countries that dominate those investments with a combined 43% share, compared to a 30% share total invested by both North and South America" (Industrial Research Institute 2017b, 21). China has increased its "total R&D investments by more than 10% annually" (Industrial Research Institute 2017b, 21). Further, China is quickly emerging as a dominant player in computing, information and communication technology (ICT), instrumentation, and military and space technology.

Elsewhere, Japan is widely considered a leader in the automotive and agricultural technology sectors; Germany is a leader in the health care, pharmaceutical, and biotechnology industries, as well as in sustainability and energy research; and France is known for its contribution to commercial aerospace R&D. In December 2017, French President Emmanuel Macron launched a climate science initiative designed to lure international researchers to France. The "Make Our Planet Great Again" initiative has recruited 18 scientists from Canada, India, the United States, and elsewhere in Europe, positioning France to take a leadership role in the world regarding climate policies (Pain 2017).

A range of environmental (many related directly to climate change) and demographic factors—including extreme weather, ocean acidification and glacial melt, energy shortages, resource scarcities, epidemics, unauthorized migration, and expanding youth and aging populations—are poised to disrupt societies, change living patterns, and increase strains on civil society, "especially where government competencies are fragile" (National Intelligence Council 2017, 207). Such issues demand both geopolitical and international science cooperation. The stakes are high. According to the National Intelligence Council's (2017, 24–25) *Global Trends: Paradox of Progress* report:

- By 2035, outdoor air pollution is projected to be the top cause of environmentally related deaths worldwide, absent implementation of new air quality policies.

- Half of the world's population will face water shortages by 2035.

- Soil degradation, or the loss of soil productivity, is occurring at rates as much as 40 times faster than new soil formation.

- Unaddressed deficiencies in national and global health systems for disease control will make infectious disease outbreaks more difficult to detect and manage and will increase the potential for epidemics.

The United Nations's Sustainable Development Goals (SDGs), codified in 2015, aim to end poverty, protect the planet, and ensure prosperity for all people (United Nations n.d.). (For more information on the SDGs, visit www.un.org/sustainabledevelopment/sustainable-development-goals.) Each SDG has specific targets to be reached over the next 15 years, and, taken together, the goals address a broad range of social and economic development issues including poverty, hunger, health, education, gender equality, water, sanitation, energy, climate change, the environment, and social justice.

According to the United Nations's "Transforming Our World: The 2030 Agenda for Sustainable Development," also known as "Agenda 2030," for those goals to be reached, governments, the private sector, civil society, and individuals must all contribute to shared outcomes (United Nations 2015). In particular, the collaborative efforts of scientists and scholars worldwide will be critical to the development of ideas, models, technology, and strategies that will allow for the attainment of such far-reaching goals. Partnership activities will add value and offer insights to key issues of global concern and impact and will serve to bridge geographical, cultural, and political boundaries. It is notable that the 17th and final SDG is a revival of global partnerships in support of the goals. Thriving partnerships across local and state actors, across nations, and among industries, nonprofit entities, local organizations, governments, and community groups are a must for the success of the remaining 16 SDGs.

The Impact of Research Partnerships

Collaboration among scientists has a long and fruitful history. Moreover, research partnerships come in all sizes, from the exchange of ideas from one scholar to another to larger-scale projects involving many scientists, equipment, and activities occurring in multiple locations. Researchers from institutions of higher education partner with many types of entities including industries, foundations, government agencies, nongovernmental organizations, national laboratories, research centers, and other academic institutions. Formal and informal interactions across academic units occur daily. Today, scholarly mobility is at an all-time high, and international research connections will inevitably expand in number and complexity (APLU Commission on International Initiatives 2017).

The following examples of international research partnerships highlight the large-scale impact such cooperation can generate.

- The European Organization for Nuclear Research (CERN) operates the largest particle physics laboratory in the world and has 22 European member states as well as associate member nations and cooperation agreements with dozens of countries. CERN has been a world leader in particle physics for half a century. More than 12,000 visiting scientists from over 70 countries and with 105 different nationalities—essentially, half of the world's particle physicists—have traveled to CERN for their research (CERN 2018). (For more information about CERN, visit home.cern/about.)

- Within the field of agricultural sciences, the International Rice Research Institute (IRRI) produced one of the first high-yielding varieties of rice that helped prevent the mass famine predicted for Asia in the 1970s. Rice is eaten by more than half of the world's population daily, making it one of the most important human foods. Today, IRRI continues to make valuable contributions to society by improving food security, reducing poverty, engaging women in science, and addressing the effects of climate change on food production. IRRI is just one of the 16 international agricultural research centers that make up the global network known as the Consultative Group for International Agricultural Research (CGIAR). The CGIAR mobilizes the world's best agricultural scientists through its research programs and centers

(CGIAR n.d.). (For more information about IRRI, visit www.cgiar. org/research/center/irri.)

- In the arena of space research, 15 nations and their constituent researchers partnered to build and operate the International Space Station (ISS) as a world-class research center in the unique environment of space. Launched in 1998, the ISS is one of the most ambitious international collaborations ever attempted: "The Program's greatest accomplishment is as much a human achievement as it is a technological one—how best to plan, coordinate, and monitor the varied activities of the Program's many international organizations" (NASA 2017). (For more information about ISS, visit www.nasa.gov/ mission_pages/station/cooperation/index.html.)

These and other multinational research partnerships have improved societies across the globe and have led to rapid increases in scholarly outputs. Research publications, especially those that include an international coauthor, have increased dramatically as a result of growing transnational partnerships. For example, in the United States, publications by a U.S.-based researcher and at least one scholar from another country have increased by 240 percent, jumping from 63,116 publications in 2001 to 216,019 in 2016 (data sourced from Elsevier Scopus on January 25, 2018). And while publications by U.S. scholars with domestic collaborators still represent approximately double the number of publications with an international coauthor, publications produced with an international coauthor often generate significantly higher-quality science (impact) and more citations than their domestic counterparts (data sourced from Elsevier Scopus on January 25, 2018).

Similarly, over the same time period, internationally coauthored research publications have grown worldwide (see figure 1). The greatest increase has been in China where scholarly publications with an international partner increased by more than 1,000 percent from 2001 to 2016 (data sourced from Elsevier Scopus on January 25, 2018). These data serve as excellent measures of the output and impact of research-based international collaborations.

Figure 1. Internationally Coauthored Publications by Country, 2001–16

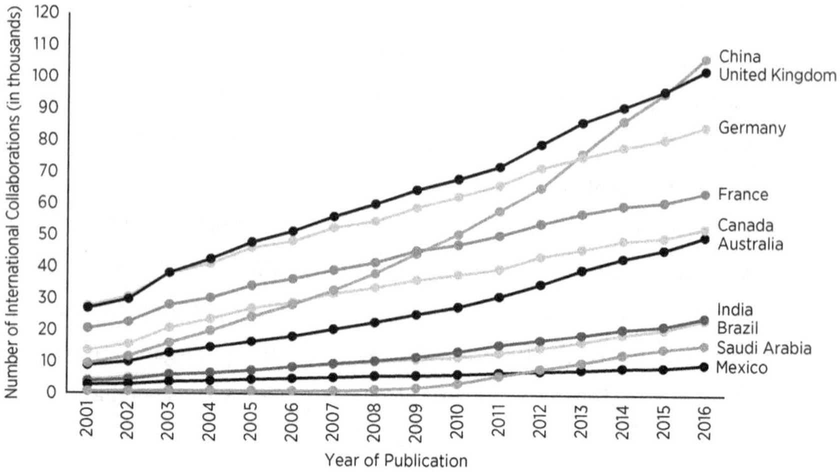

Source: Data sourced from Elsevier Scopus on July 26, 2018.

In addition to publications, international research partnerships often generate proposals for external funding, grants, contracts, scholarly awards (e.g., Nobel Prizes, United Nations's Intercultural Innovation Awards, Fulbright Awards), and innovation that lead to successful patent applications and the commercialization of technology. Research collaboration among international partners allows researchers to take advantage of compatible expertise, equipment, exchanges, and training, which accelerates the discovery process.

Establishment of Institutional Research Partnerships

International collaboration among scientists often occurs organically and stems from a desire at the individual level to work with others who bring a different perspective, cultural lens, history, language, or values to the project. Universities often leave faculty to their own devices and personal connections to establish research relationships with international colleagues. At the institutional level, the articulation of a strategy for international engagement can help leaders prioritize partnerships, allocate resources and talent, and communicate both the opportunities to researchers and the successes to the broader community.

Motivations for a Partnership Strategy

The ideal international research partnership advances discovery and provides solutions to complex challenges by harnessing diverse perspectives and approaches for a common goal. Successful international partnerships require an investment of time at the outset to establish concrete goals and to build confidence and trust among partners. Viable relationships depend on identifying partners with complementary expertise or skills, compatible academic cultures, access to networks and funds, the ability to adapt to changing circumstances, and a record of successful collaboration. On the other hand, the duplication of talents or an imbalance in skills, competition for leadership, failure to share risk, or a "controlling" partner or a partner who "collects" partners (without true commitment) does little to cultivate true collaboration.

The factors that motivate an institution to develop intentional partnerships vary widely. In a 2015 global survey managed by the Institute of International Education and the Freie Universität Berlin, the top reasons that surveyed institutions of higher education gave for investing in strategic partnerships included improving research capacity, the quality of research outputs, and expanded opportunities for researchers (Kuder 2015). These types of partnerships are the result of formal alliances where partners "share resources and leverage complementary strengths to achieve defined common objectives" (Banks, Siebe-Herbig, and Norton 2016, xi). These partnerships include significant research initiatives that are multidimensional and may include student/faculty exchange, dual or joint academic degrees, study abroad opportunities, community engagement, industry connections, joint funding, and other indicators of a deep commitment among the partners.

ENHANCING GLOBAL IMPACT

The driving force behind some international research partnerships is the opportunity to work collaboratively to produce gains on a global scale. Research partnerships are an ideal way to find new and different ways of approaching societal challenges. Through partnerships, universities can gain access to technology and infrastructure unavailable at the home institution, the ability to share the high cost of research with another organization, access to new and different funding streams, and complementary expertise and compatible research goals. These partnerships leverage the research expertise housed in one institution with complementary knowledge from other institutions and entities to fuel new discoveries and innovations that support the United Nations's SDGs.

International research collaboration facilitates the extension and application of knowledge to a broad audience. For example, the University of Exeter in England and The University of Queensland (UQ) in Australia have established and invested in a partnership designed to bolster both institutions' global research impact. The partnership is intended to incentivize collaborative "research of the highest quality, boost industry and business collaboration, and publish high-level policy reports designed to inform and shape key government initiatives across the globe" (University of Exeter 2017). The outcomes of international research partnerships can serve the needs of decisionmakers and policymakers across academia, industries, and governments, which can have widespread impact on the present day and the future.

STRENGTHENING SIGNATURE AREAS OF EXPERTISE

Often, an institution of higher education will organize a partnership strategy around interdisciplinary areas where the institution already has research interest and capacity in order to further improve its global reputation. For a university to claim to be a leader in a certain field, the institution must be home to key researchers or combinations of researchers, materials of a certain importance (e.g., archives, biological samples, equipment), and an established record of high-impact discovery. International research partnerships help to secure these contributing factors that can lead to added prominence within the scientific fields. Common signature areas of concentration for international research include climate, infectious diseases, conflict resolution, food and water security, clean energy, human health and safety, and other topics that reflect the United Nations's SDGs. Signature areas of research can also be quite novel and singular, such as optics or cybersecurity.

International research partnerships can promote engagement between institutions that are leaders in overlapping areas of research expertise. For example, the International Consortium of Universities for the Study of Biodiversity and the Environment (iCUBE) has brought together a group of top-tier research universities representing Australia, Brunei, England, Germany, Singapore, South Korea, and the United States to form a consortium capable of addressing a wide variety of issues related to biodiversity, climate change, and the environment. (For more information about iCUBE, visit icubeconsortium. org/index.php/about-menu.) By sharing knowledge and resources across leading institutions, advances in the field are supported and developed in an optimal setting of collaboration.

ESTABLISHING A FOOTPRINT IN GEOGRAPHIC AREAS OF FOCUS

Regional interests are another aspect to the motivation and direction behind partnership development. Most research universities have identified geographic locations of strategic importance and locations of emerging opportunity by assessing research strengths, areas where faculty are already engaged, funding opportunities, industry interest, and other factors. An international research partnership can allow an institution to have a presence in a key region for field research and other experiential work, whether that is through an exchange agreement or a physical facility. Cooperative agreements can also give researchers access to more remote destinations and communities that would otherwise be unreachable for new and emerging studies.

For example, The Ohio State University (Ohio State) has established key "Global Gateways" in countries of cultural and economic importance to the university and to industry groups in Ohio. Ohio State methodically planned its global reach: "The Gateway concept was born out of the need to be more strategic in the university's international engagement….establishing a physical presence in key locations around the world [that] would enable Ohio State to develop broader and deeper ties" (Brustein and Miller 2011, 2). The Global Gateways have provided the opportunity for Ohio State researchers to engage and partner with a new range of constituencies (Brustein and Miller 2011, 2). International research partnerships can help to establish or expand an institution's reach within a strategic world region or demographic.

Development of an International Research Partnership

There are a multitude of recipes for international partnership development. Each university must chart its own course and the organizational strategies that support international research endeavors. Romo (2015, 2016) highlights several key stages of a well-defined strategic research partnership plan:

- Identify the university's strategic international research mission by seeking input (and ideally, consensus) from faculty/researchers, administrators, and staff across the institution.

- Establish and communicate the institution's research strengths across disciplines, facilities, and equipment.

- Seek international partners with assets that are complementary to the identified research strengths and geographic priorities of the university and choose partners with enthusiasm for collaboration.

- Consider the history of interaction with the partner, the level of trust among senior leadership, and the willingness of each partner to devote energy and resources to making the research collaboration(s) a success.

- Appoint a central coordinating body or unit at the institutional level, identify an office or offices responsible for supporting and facilitating international research initiatives, and dedicate the necessary space and resources.

- Establish clear coordination at the institutional level and integrate planning involving key departments and units to encourage cooperation and minimize power conflicts. This is especially important for large-scale projects or initiatives involving multiple disciplines, colleges, faculties, or centers.

- Define decisionmaking roles and responsibilities. Clarify who decides the assignment of resources, the priorities, and the level and types of collaboration expected.

- Review the status and activity of research partnerships across the institution according to a predetermined schedule (annually, for example).

- Conduct face-to-face visits between partners to establish and maintain trust and enthusiasm for the partnership. Leverage technology to advance relationships through virtual meetings, document and data sharing, and other points of connection.

- Examine the relationship between the university and the wider community, including consulates and embassies, governments (and their agencies), local businesses and industries, national and international organizations, and alumni.

- Recognize that time, flexibility, and persistence are required to sustain international research partnerships and initiatives.

Research collaboration involves a higher level of complexity when investigators work across national borders in relationships that may include the purchase and use of equipment, creation of new technology, employment of foreign staff and payments to foreign nations, the maintenance of multiple research sites and labs, and the creation of multinational consortia. For international research partnerships to flourish, a formal agreement or memorandum of understanding (MOU) that describes mutual interests, identifies the benefits for each collaborator and organization, ensures that collective resources are sufficient to achieve objectives and that the parties to the agreement have the authority to commit resources, and clearly articulates the outcomes of the partnership is an excellent way to make sure that all stakeholders are on the same page from the very beginning of the partnership. A strong research partnership will address at the outset potentially thorny issues involving data management, timelines, ethics, research integrity, conflict of interest, rights to authorship, ownership of intellectual property, export controls, and the transfer of information and equipment, among other potential conflicts (Holbrook and Caruson 2017). Ultimately, however, trust among partners is the most important predictor of success and sustainability.

Sustainable Research Partnerships

Sustaining successful international research partnerships takes work. According to the National Academies, "As science and technology capabilities grow around the world, U.S.-based organizations are finding that international collaborations and partnerships provide unique opportunities to enhance research and training. At the same time, significant obstacles exist to smooth collaboration across national borders" (Sloan and Arrison 2011, 16). A number of hurdles associated with differences in operating procedures at the institutional level, laws and regulations, cultural norms, and access to technology and equipment are discussed in detail in the next section.

The Global Research Council (GRC) is actively taking steps to address some of the barriers to international collaboration. GRC is a virtual organization comprised of the heads of science and engineering funding agencies from around the world, such as the U.S. National Science Foundation, the Japan Society for the Promotion of Science, the National Natural Science Foundation of China, and the Natural Sciences and Engineering Research Council of Canada, among others. Members of the GRC are dedicated to sharing data and best practices that promote high-quality collaboration among funding agencies worldwide.

Recently, agency heads recognized that national funding agencies are managing an increasing number of international programs to facilitate mobility and research collaboration. As a result, "GRC participants identified the potential to improve international research collaboration by examining and adopting practices that reduce administrative complexity, remove barriers to participation, and support collaboration" (Global Research Council 2017, 3). (For more information on GRC and its practices, visit www.globalresearch-council.org/about/global-research-council.) GRC offers a series of principles that help to overcome some of the identified obstacles. As history has shown, partnerships become more vulnerable to pitfalls at the point where collaborative research is made operational through the allocation or transfer of funds, the specification of deliverables, and the development of concrete research plans (Sloan and Arrison 2011, 20). These and other challenges to sustaining international research partnerships are discussed below.

Challenges to International Collaboration

Barriers that inhibit smooth international research collaborations include differences in laws; unique regulations and reporting requirements of a country (or lack thereof); inadequate or different levels of human subject protections across nations; and political, economic, and social conditions that create risk. To avoid misunderstandings that may arise from possible differences in expectations among partners (i.e., academic, industry, and government), the topic of research ethics and integrity and the standards of research compliance must be addressed formally when the partnership is initially formed. It is also important to ensure mutual interests and benefits at the outset regarding issues such as data management plans (e.g., collection, storage, and security); the management and storage of research materials (e.g., tissue, cell lines, and reagents); potential conflicts of interest; rights to authorship; ownership of intellectual property; and expectations of each partner in terms of commitment of people/researchers, time, resources, and administrative support.

INSTITUTIONAL CHALLENGES

Two common institutional challenges associated with establishing a global research support operation are that (a) no single unit "owns" the issue; and that (b) institutions have limited resources and many competing priorities. Research collaboration requires the support and organization of multiple offices and stakeholders across campus; it cannot be "owned" by a single unit because of the far-reaching impacts on personnel and resources. Silos between units may result in a lack of coordination, or duplication of efforts, which will inhibit the partnership from succeeding for the long term.

Furthermore, the institution itself may have competing priorities that can lead to an underdeveloped strategy for global engagement. Senior leaders may not have been educated about the benefits of a global research support system and the risks of under-resourcing support services. There may be a hesitation to challenge senior management's assumptions that global endeavors are already adequately supported, or a reluctance to require more of researchers' time in terms of compliance and reporting. Partnerships depend on support from all levels of the institution, from the faculty to the top leadership.

The university's global brand is at stake, and its ability to effectively manage the risks associated with an international research portfolio will influence the university's ability to advertise its global successes. Lack of a support system and adequate resources for global research partnerships can produce frustration among researchers and staff and create situations where individuals take matters into their own hands—for better or worse. Crises happen when there is no mechanism (or support unit) in place to monitor compliance, manage project complexities, and assist researchers.

LEGAL CHALLENGES

Legal issues in international research collaboration require the involvement of legal expertise on both sides of the partnership to evaluate whether the objectives of all parties are realistic, understood, and aligned. For example, implementation of the General Data Protection Regulation (GDPR) as it pertains to citizens of the European Union and related research agreements is an area where legal counsel can be critical. Legal advice is also essential to decisions regarding tax liabilities, the transfer of money, overseas employment, immigration and work visas, contracting and subawards to foreign entities, the shipping of research materials, and rules for the disposition of assets, equipment, and vehicles when the project concludes.

The ownership of intellectual property (IP) is one of the most contentious legal issues that must be addressed when forming an international research collaboration (Sloan and Alper 2014). Universities manage the ownership rights of IP generated by faculty, students, and staff through the licensing of new technology, commercialization, and formation of start-up companies. There are added layers of complexity when students are among the inventors, when the inventors work at multiple universities, or when government and industry partners have rights associated with the research and the creation of IP.

Bigger challenges are present when the partners are from different nations. Country-specific laws and regulations govern intellectual property; IP laws are primarily national and have not been internationally harmonized. Additionally, research universities have codes of conduct in place regarding collaborative projects that involve possible IP generation. Universities should have a dedicated office with contract managers who oversee IP and technology transfer matters. In certain cases, the complexity of a project may necessitate outside legal counsel.

The key is to establish expectations regarding IP ownership and management *before* the project begins—at the initial stages of partnership development.

A separate contract may be necessary to clearly establish who (what entity) owns (or will own) what. Institutions must conduct due diligence before IP or licensing issues arise, and they must be prepared for a variety of interpretations regarding ownership. Researchers will need assistance navigating the labyrinth of rules and regulations regarding IP assets and rights (i.e., patents, copyrights, and trademarks) and licensing agreements. The same can be said for export control regimes and patent applications, which are also country specific (Holbrook and Caruson 2017).

It is also important to note that funding agencies take cross-border compliance issues seriously. Regulators from around the world have grown sophisticated concerning their ability to exercise oversight. Partners should articulate a process for dispute resolution before one is needed.

CULTURAL CHALLENGES

Culture can influence attitudes and practices regarding research and ethics, such as in the use of human and animal subjects; participation of minorities, children, or indigenous populations in research and clinical trials; inclusion of graduate students and postdoctoral associates; IP ownership; export control issues; financial management of grants; decisions regarding the publication of findings; and the formality of agreements with partners. National boundaries often impact the rules for creating an agreement and how a partnership is carried out in practice (Sloan and Alper 2014, 4).

Cultural differences can be as complex as the legal framework under which agreements are formulated or as simple as the meanings attributed to a particular word. There may be differences in cultural norms that must be navigated. For example, faculty responsibilities regarding teaching compared with research can vary tremendously from nation to nation—faculty in many countries have heavy teaching loads—as can expectations about timelines and how quickly (or slowly) project components will be completed. Styles of communication vary from direct and geared to quick decisionmaking to indirect and focused on achieving group consensus. The degree to which verbal confrontation is tolerated, and the means of expressing opposition, is subject to cultural norms. Additionally, across regions of the world, there are divergent opinions regarding the role of women in society and the level of interest in gender and racial equality and diversity (Metcalfe and Day 2016). For all of these reasons, institutions should take care to engage their international office early and often in research collaborations, as staff with backgrounds and experience in understanding and interpreting cultural differences can help keep projects on track and expectations aligned.

TECHNOLOGY CHALLENGES

There are also information technology (IT) challenges when working to develop and sustain relationships with international partners. Technology and communication capacities vary by country, and that can have a large impact on research outputs. Internet access; the reliability and availability of technologies such as DSL, fiber, cable, and wireless; and the availability of computers, tablets, teleconferencing equipment, and other types of IT hardware are all factors to consider. Research collaborations require active and ongoing communication between partner institutions, no matter how that communication is achieved.

Differences also exist in terms of the speed of connectivity and the cost of broadband services. Broadband speed and prices (monthly) vary dramatically around the world from just over U.S.$5.00 in Iran to U.S.$66.00 in the United States to a high of nearly U.S.$1,000 in the West African nation of Burkina Faso (McCarthy 2017). Power outages affect the ability to communicate, and a lack of IT infrastructure can complicate file sharing, damage the security of information, and generally slow down the progress of research partnerships.

These technological, cultural, legal, and institutional challenges can hinder the research partnership from remaining productive and sustainable. However, there are best practices that can be implemented and issues that can be addressed during the partnership development stage that will enable the research collaboration to succeed.

Considerations for Success

Initiating and sustaining an international research partnership requires tax, legal, and administrative considerations. Identifying potential risk exposure to the university and its researchers is critical, as is the need to explicitly document expectations, roles, and responsibilities. The following topics should be carefully considered and addressed before research activities begin in order to prevent the dissolution of the partnership before outcomes are met.

- What is the extent of the alignment of the proposed partnership with the university's research goals and strengths?

- Is there already an established partnership agreement or research MOU with the intended collaborator(s)?

- Is the partner country, university, or researchers on an export control list or anti-boycott list or have Office of Foreign Assets (OFAC) sanctions?

- What is the scope of work to be done domestically? What is the scope of work to be done internationally?

- What types of activities are anticipated? Are there clinical activities planned? Will human or animal subjects be utilized? Will there be costs to these activities? What are the relevant regulations or policies governing research that involves human or animal subjects? Are all members of the research team familiar with the country-specific policies regarding these types of activities?

- Is there a research administration unit or office at each partner institution involved in the project? What is the capacity of the research administration unit at each partner institution?

- What is the funding source for the project? What are the reporting requirements of the sponsor? Are there any expectations from partner entities regarding investment in their institutions? Who is contributing what to the partnership, and will equipment, facilities, goods, services, or other materials become the final property of the foreign partner?

- Will an international subcontract be needed to accomplish the research objectives?

- What are the staffing requirements? Will university faculty, staff, or students be present in the partner country? If so, for how long (how many days)? Will any staff be relocated? For how long? How will staff be paid? Will any stipends be offered? Will the research project engage any external individuals as employees of independent contractors in the foreign country? Will a human resources vendor be necessary?

- Depending on the number and amount of time staff spend abroad, will it be necessary to establish a formal legal presence in the partner country? Will foreign-based counsel be required for legal advising?

- What kind of fiscal systems need to be put in place, such as bank accounts, invoicing procedures, purchasing cards, etc.? How will partner country banking policies and laws affect how funds are transferred and made available?

- Are there any partner country insurance requirements that will apply to any aspect of the research project?

- What type of laboratory and office space is necessary? What equipment, furniture, supplies, and other items are required?

- What are the IT needs? Will any technology or communications equipment be shipped to or from a foreign location?

- Will there be any IP involved in the project? What entity will own the rights to the IP? How will the IP be protected and made available to participants at the conclusion of the partnership or project? Is it likely that a patent will be applied for? Is any commercialization of the research anticipated?

It is impossible to overstate the importance of trust and frank communication among partners. Advance negotiation and open communication will ensure that all parties share a similar vision and expectation and that the collective resources are adequate to achieve the research objectives. Collaborators can always choose to begin with a one-year pilot project to determine mutual interest, expectations, and objectives. If the venture goes smoothly and the stakeholders remain engaged, the project can be extended or even expanded.

On-Campus Stakeholders and Allies

The adoption and implementation of policies that will advance international research partnerships are dependent on highly visible advocates with the ability to influence the mission, vision, and strategic goals of the university (Holbrook and Caruson 2017). A vocal president/chancellor/rector can set the stage for the prioritization of international research, with the support of the provost/senior vice president for academic affairs, the senior international officer (SIO), and the vice president for research (VPR), as well as other key leadership officials (e.g., deans, heads of faculties and their equivalents). Ideally, the individuals in these key positions will possess an awareness and appreciation for both the research enterprise and international engagement.

Far too often, however, administrators from offices that either directly or indirectly support international research collaborate infrequently, rarely share personal or physical space, have limited knowledge about each other's day-to-day activities, and may not speak the same "language" in terms of priorities, evaluation metrics, and business practices. More opportunities to connect administrators in the research enterprise and those representing international initiatives must be created so that they can form personal relationships and identify ways for fostering greater cooperation between the two offices.

Once the partnership agreement is signed and in effect, the larger tasks of implementing, managing, promoting, and sustaining a robust international research operation rest with a broad coalition of units on campus. Key stakeholders include university and college trustees and governing boards; the leader of the institution or university system; constituent organizations or campuses and their respective oversight boards and leaders; academic departments and faculties; individual researchers, scientists, and staff; students; and the broader university community, including industries.

Trustees, governing boards, and senior leaders have a responsibility to ensure that institutional partnerships provide value to the university and, ideally, enhance global prestige. It is incumbent upon colleges, departments, and their associated faculties to sustain research partnerships through the exchange of doctoral students between labs, regular communication and face-to-face visits, as well as joint conference presentations, publications, and grant proposals, to name a few activities. Many universities have established offices of corporate relations to provide a "front door" for industries interested in partnering with academia. These offices can help researchers connect with research opportunities in the industry sector, domestically and abroad. Industry connections often provide more than research contracts; they can open the door to student internships and eventual employment.

Creating an environment or ecosystem for international research requires collaboration across university units. Successful partnerships rely as much on effective internal relationships as they do on engagement with external stakeholders (West 2012; Proctor 2016). International research is often considered to be the primary concern of the central research office, but global research projects require the input of many units across an organization, including the offices of finance, travel, compliance, legal, technology, purchasing, payments, human resources, risk management, and marketing and communication, as seen in figure 2.

Figure 2. Internal Stakeholders of the Global Research Ecosystem

Source: Holbrook and Caruson (2017). Reprinted with permission from USF World and the University of South Florida.

The responsibilities involved in implementing partnerships are often distributed across an institution, but, in many cases, there are limited opportunities to share knowledge and brainstorm better ways of doing business. In order for global research to flourish, administrators and staff across organizational units must value and understand each other's contributions to research engagement, and they must also identify collaborative ways to advance internationally funded and focused research. Clarity regarding the responsibilities of each stakeholder in the partnership relationship is crucial for consistent, productive communication. It is valuable for institutions to think strategically

Global Research Tool Kit

In 2017, with funding from the Society for Research Administrators International's Big Ideas Initiative, the University of South Florida worked with collaborators from more than 30 countries to develop an online global research tool kit (for more information, visit www.lib.usf.edu/GlobalResearchToolkit). The contents of the tool kit are organized around key themes and strategies for international research project success. The goal of the tool kit is to equip researchers and administrators with information and access to a global forum for information and knowledge sharing.

A related 2017 survey of more than 1,000 research administrators, faculty, and other associated professionals from around the world found that international research responsibilities are more than an "occasional" job function for the majority of respondents (Caruson 2017). The most challenging aspects of working with international partners were reported to include:

- Navigating differences in regulations such as export control mandates (62 percent);
- Managing subcontracts/awards (53 percent);
- Audit and compliance issues (45 percent);
- Matters relating to the management of intellectual property (43 percent); and
- Overall award management (42 percent).

Furthermore, the survey revealed that although 77 percent of respondents work for an institution or organization that "values" or "highly values" global research, only 22 percent reported their capacity to manage international research projects/partnerships as "sophisticated" or "good," and an equal number (22 percent) reported a "need for improvement" and capacity building (Caruson 2017). The results of the survey provide additional evidence for the establishment of global research support units and networks that serve to enhance an institution's ability to develop, sustain, and expand global research partnerships.

Additional examples of online research tool kits managed by universities include the University of California system (www.ucgo.org), UPenn Global Support Services (global.upenn.edu/gss), and the University of Washington's Global Operations Support (finance.uw.edu/globalsupport/home).

about how to create a support system for global research that enfranchises many experts. How to best do this depends on the particular institution, its culture, organization, and resources.

There are many excellent examples of how universities have designed offices and programs to support international research endeavors that play to the disciplinary strengths of faculty and the strategic priorities of the institution. Dedicated offices that provide international research support can be situated within the research area, the international unit, or within a college, or it may be organized as a stand-alone unit that bridges the two primary offices (research and international) and has independent budget authority. Other options include a dedicated unit or department, a university-wide steering committee, a staff-level working group for operational issues, and a "community of practice" or "network" of experts who meet virtually and face-to-face.

The creation of handbooks, project start-up guides, and templates, as well as training programs for faculty and staff go a long way in building capacity among stakeholders. Built-in flags or notices in university software systems for personnel, travel, proposal development, program tracking, and international travel forms and risk and safety monitoring can help to pave the way for success. Knowing when to bring in outside consultants or legal expertise is also critical. Successful global research universities capitalize on the talent and experience of faculty, staff, students, administrators, and supporters to create and maintain a high-impact international research enterprise.

Encouragement and Recognition of Faculty Engagement

Faculty researchers are the backbone of international research collaborations and serve as allies for institutional partnerships. Universities can be creative in designing avenues for soliciting researchers' participation in international collaborations, partnerships, and consortia—as well as in the ways the universities choose to reward and recognize international engagement by faculty (Holbrook and Caruson 2017). Working internationally and successfully can be time-consuming and labor-intensive. Researchers who have invested in international collaborations and partnerships should be recognized for their efforts and rewarded for their accomplishments at the time of career advancement.

REWARDING INTERNATIONALIZATION ACTIVITIES

In the tenure and promotion process, most universities factor in activities that contribute to the academic reputation of a faculty member at the national and international levels. However, fewer institutions define international engagement as a separate category for evaluation. Faculty recognition, according to clearly designed career advancement metrics, is at the center of any institutional mechanism to encourage international research engagement. Including international activities among the ways a faculty member can be recognized in tenure and promotion within the traditional standards of teaching, research, and service does not add a new category, but rather a new measure of achievement within any one of the existing categories. In lieu of a formal reference to the value of international research engagement in tenure and promotion criteria, guidelines for promotion should be aligned with the university's strategic priorities or goals.

In addition to carving out space for international research within guidelines and requirements for career advancement, universities must invest resources into programs that support international research partnerships. Faculty members need resources in the form of time, funding, and support services. Opportunities for leave time or sabbaticals that extend over two semesters are especially useful for international mobility. Time away from the home campus must be accompanied by the continuation of full or partial salary. Funds are also needed for the costs associated with international travel; for required matching funds to obtain grants to conduct research abroad; to recruit international scholars and postdoctoral researchers; and to organize and conduct programs, conferences, and workshops that attract international participation.

FUNDING INTERNATIONALIZATION ACTIVITIES

Many institutions offer internal seed grants that are designed to catalyze and sustain international partnerships. The funding might be used for visits or small workshops to formulate joint research projects, develop external proposal submissions, or expand existing collaborations. Partnership-building funds can be targeted to a specific discipline or "global challenge," such as infectious diseases or water and food security. Partner universities or organizations can demonstrate their commitment to the partnership by dedicating resources, including earmarked funding, personnel (e.g., shared students or postdoctoral researchers), and access to specialized equipment, labs, or library materials such as special collections.

These grants, or other financial incentives, help international teams of researchers become more competitive candidates for external funding by allowing for data collection, proof of concept, and determination of project viability or expansion. Ideally, internal grant funds should lead to proposals to private foundations and the various national research councils including the National Science Foundation, the National Institutes of Health, United States Agency for International Development, the British Council, the Alliance Française, the Alexander von Humboldt Foundation, and the European Commission, which includes the Marie Skłodowska-Curie actions (an excellent option for researcher mobility), as well as other funding opportunities for researchers from specific regions including China, Japan, and North America, among others (de Grijs 2015). The Fulbright Program is a valuable avenue for building research partnerships between institutions.

FACILITATING INTERNATIONALIZATION ACTIVITIES

Workshops and mentoring for faculty and students interested in certain types of international awards are especially useful and will increase the success rate of proposals and applications. It is wise to collect information about faculty successes—with grant proposals, projects, funders, and honors and awards—to identify individuals who can serve as mentors, application reviewers, and workshop leaders and participants.

As international mobility increases, researchers need easy access to information regarding travel, including but not limited to health and immunization information, security updates and travel advisories, in-country emergency contact information, foreign per diem rates, host country business practices, gifting and cultural advice, and country and city guides. Online guides for countries and cities frequently visited are helpful, as is the expertise of an in-house international risk and safety analyst or officer.

A number of universities have identified "ambassadors" among the faculty who are willing to serve as representatives to faculty colleagues and administrators regarding particular countries or cultures. Alumni living abroad (i.e., former domestic and international students) also serve an important role. They may be able to connect researchers with in-county or local resources, and they may offer homestays or other types of support.

More technical guidance on managing faculty internationalization efforts can be accessed from the National Association of College and University Business Officers (NACUBO) International Resource Center, the University Risk Management and Insurance Association (URMIA), and the Government-University-Industry Research Roundtable (GUIRR), in combination with the expertise of an international tax adviser or consulting firm. With external and internal sources of support, international research activities can be encouraged, promoted, and rewarded.

Approaches to Tracking and Evaluating the Impact of International Research Partnerships

Thousands of scientists and researchers are currently conducting excellent collaborative science, technology, and innovation research projects around the world. However, it has been noted that many university leaders do not readily know where their faculty members conduct research overseas or the degree of their research engagement. Because most international networks of scientists are self-organizing, many U.S. universities lack effective means to capture and communicate information about such international research linkages. No national clearinghouse exists to showcase these assets for science engagement and diplomacy. Moreover, many U.S. universities do not immediately think of U.S. embassies and consulates as resources and, as a result, fail to share their foreign activities with these potential linkage points. Some universities, however, are starting to build the capacity to map their international networks with a range of tools (Colglazier and Lyons 2014).

Asset Mapping

Data are essential to documenting the breadth and depth of global engagement. Often, there is conventional wisdom about areas of research strength or program activity, but when data are collected systematically, the results can be surprising. The process of asset mapping reveals important information for partnership strategies, including discipline areas of research strength, activity, and interest; geographic areas of importance (e.g., locations of student mobility, faculty research collaboration); the proportion of external funding that is internationally sourced; the level of grant activity that is international; the number and types of awards and honors bestowed upon faculty and staff; and faculty expertise in foreign languages and cultures.

The first step to asset mapping is to determine what data sources or databases already exist at the university and what information can be accessed to populate new datasets with relative ease. Connecting with colleagues in the university libraries and the IT department is important because these entities traditionally manage subscription databases and have expertise in developing and maintaining them. For example, universities will want to take stock of the honors and awards their faculty have received for research endeavors and then use that data to set goals for future accomplishments and to implement practices and policies that encourage faculty engagement and success. The partnerships that develop from Fulbright exchanges, for instance, may lead to notable awards and highly competitive, funded projects.

Universities can develop lists, datasets, and online and interactive databases that come in all shapes and sizes. There is no "one-size-fits-all" solution. Some products for data collection and asset mapping can be purchased off the shelf through vendors and then customized by the university. A number of universities have developed their own systems and platforms, some of which are accessible to only members of the individual institution. Ideally, universities will orient some aspects of the asset mapping exercises outward, giving the public the opportunity to view and explore the specific university's international footprint. A narrow data collection effort may evolve into a larger exercise, depending on the needs and goals of the institution.

Metrics for Assessing International Research Engagement

Data can be used to articulate metrics that provide a data-driven justification for investing in international scholarship and research partnerships. Such information is beneficial not just to the research and international offices, but to other university units as well. For example, performance measures can be used to recognize and reward faculty and students (or units) for achievement in the international research arena. Data can also be used to analyze the productivity of partnerships.

Metrics can be captured by unit (e.g., faculties, departments, colleges) or by topic (e.g., sustainability, energy, security) to facilitate assessments of return on investment, strategic planning, and the measurement of progress toward goals. This type of analysis is critical to assessing the goodness of fit with international partners and for identifying and promoting partnerships in countries and regions of strategic opportunity. Metrics for international research can also be used for student recruitment and fundraising initiatives.

As international research and engagement emerges as a top priority for universities around the world, institutions need tools to measure and benchmark the impact and outcomes of international collaborations. For example, a study funded by the National Science Foundation (NSF) of five public universities selected for geographic and academic diversities (Colorado State University, Kansas State University, Michigan State University, University of North Texas, and Washington State University) provided a testing ground for the development of a set of international research indicators (Arasu 2016). The metrics were associated with personnel, grants, expenditures, coauthored publications, citation impact, article downloads, and co-inventions with international collaborators for the 2008–12 period. Data for the study were obtained from a commissioned project with Elsevier's Research Intelligence Unit and Scopus database resources, as well as from each of the participating institutions. According to NSF's International Research Evaluation Metrics study, all five institutions showed that at least a third of their total publications involved international coauthors, and the impact of those publications were significantly higher than the institutional and world average (Arasu 2016). The number of grant applications, awards, and coauthored publications with an international collaborator(s) increased over the 2008–12 period for each of the five universities under evaluation (Arasu 2016). Other metrics varied by university and over time.

In addition to the NSF study, Snowball Metrics represents a similar university-driven effort to identify and evaluate national and international research indicators. Snowball Metrics was initiated in 2010 by research-intensive universities in the United Kingdom, in partnership with Elsevier. The original UK universities have since been joined by a U.S. working group and an Australia/New Zealand working group. The goal of Snowball Metrics is to "develop clearly defined metrics in close collaboration with the research community in order to help universities establish institutional strategies on the basis of their research performance" (Plume 2014). (For more information about Snowball Metrics, visit www.snowballmetrics.com.) The output of Snowball Metrics is a set of mutually agreed upon and tested methodologies, called "recipes," that relate to metrics associated with inputs, processes, outputs, and outcomes. The goal is that the metrics "become global standards that enable institutional benchmarking and cover the entire spectrum of research activities" (Snowball Metrics n.d.).

Not all of the Snowball Metrics are relevant for international research, but of particular interest are those associated with international collaboration and the impact of collaboration. For example, Queen's University Belfast noticed that, despite being ahead of its peers on growth in scholarly publications, the institution was lagging in citations, which account for a large proportion of the data used to calculate global rankings. A deeper analysis showed that although international collaboration was high, it was limited to primarily European partners. The university launched an outreach campaign to its researchers that included broader development of international networks and collaborations, which in turn helped to raise the quality and impact of its research publications (Colledge 2017).

Institutions interested in developing and adopting metrics designed to measure the value and impact of international research partnerships will need to consider the level of access to data, the ease of collection, and the quality of available data, as well as the level of resources (personnel and funding) available for such an endeavor. A quantitative, objective assessment of research performance and productivity is best matched with a deep, qualitative assessment of an institution's research environment, researchers, and strategic priorities. Data of this type contribute to a university's reputation and prestige and can be used to identify areas of research strength, critical mass, and signature expertise.

Evaluation of International Research Partnerships

Equally important to understanding a university's international research engagement is a thorough assessment of its international partnerships (e.g., general agreements, student exchanges, project-specific MOUs), including not only the "type" of agreement, but the scope of the agreement, the activities associated with the agreement, and any scholarships or fellowships that researchers might use to engage with partner organizations. Mapping a university's partnerships and monitoring the activities associated with them is critical. Some partnerships will be discipline- or unit-specific and, thus, narrow in the scope of activities, but others will comprise varying levels of faculty and student involvement.

The University of Queensland (UQ) in Australia has one of the most sophisticated systems for monitoring and evaluating existing and potential partnerships. The university's Partner Engagement Framework (PEF), coupled with its Country Engagement Framework, measures the effectiveness and success of international engagement with clearly defined, data-driven metrics. The university's international engagement profile is the result of strategic partnerships with people and organizations across industries, governments, philanthropy, alumni, and higher education. The PEF focuses on regions and countries that have been given priority status due to their potential for deep, productive, and sustainable relationships.

The effectiveness of UQ's engagement strategy is measured using indicators related to various aspects of institutional collaboration and linkages. The PEF allows the university to assess areas of current strength, potential for future initiatives, and areas where further development is needed to maximize mutual benefit. Thirteen indicators within three categories (Discovery, Engagement, and Learning) inform partnership evaluation, including the volume, impact, and breadth of joint publications; funded joint research projects; the recruitment of staff; and student exchange and inbound study abroad. The use of a sophisticated process for evidence-based decisionmaking allows the university to continually identify highly engaged partners, the degree of partnership engagement across a given country, how best to leverage existing partnerships, and how to broaden and deepen engagements, including whether to invest in new partnerships. (For more information on The University of Queensland's Partner Engagement Framework, visit global-engagement.uq.edu.au/uq-staff/partner-engagement-framework.)

As another example, the University of South Florida (USF) has an extensive, data-driven, online, and interactive system for mapping and evaluating international research partnerships. USF's Global Discovery Hub database, commonly referred to as the "Hub," features the university's international partnerships, detailed information regarding faculty activities across the globe, and data on student mobility and alumni. (For more information on the University of South Florida's Global Discovery Hub, visit www.usf.edu/gdh.) One of the attributes of the Hub that generates the greatest interest is the faculty module. The Hub contains over 1,200 faculty profiles, tracking more than 2,000 international activities from across the USF system.

The implementation of the Hub allows the university to document, recognize, reward, and trumpet the faculty's diverse international research endeavors, as well as the success of its research partnerships. The Hub has made it possible to better connect faculty with targeted funding announcements, identify regional and country experts, improve success rates for international awards (e.g., Fulbright Awards), and connect researchers with collaborators at partner institutions. Within the Hub, members of the USF community may access an array of resources for international research, including funding sources, global partnership information, proposal development services, travel information, country and city guides, and links to guidance regarding managing risk and safety and export control practices.

International business partners and relationships with international corporations and industries, both locally and abroad, are also important to consider.

These relationships open the door to funding for researchers and experiential learning for students. International agreements across university research parks or business incubators provide an avenue for soft landings for businesses looking for new markets and opportunities for collaboration and innovation between academics and industry professionals. For all of these reasons, including international industry connections in an inventory can help an institution understand and benefit from the full spectrum of global research connections.

Efforts should be made to track international sponsored projects (e.g., grants and contracts) as well as externally funded projects that are international in scope. This is a critically important metric for evaluating the return on investment of international research partnerships. Such an assessment will require cooperation between the international and research offices (and other units) for accuracy. In addition, university advancement offices should be able to report gifts and fundraising efforts that support international partnerships.

A Look Toward the Future

Basic and applied research conducted at institutions of higher education across the world will continue to advance discovery and, ultimately, answer questions that have yet to be determined. Academic institutions serve as the world's primary driver of basic research. In the United States, roughly 60 percent of basic research is conducted at universities (Industrial Research Institute 2017a, 12). The influence of academic research extends beyond the campus: "Academia is also an invaluable resource for research staff in industry and government labs, along with leaders in government and industry through its graduate and post-graduate programs" (Industrial Research Institute 2017a, 12).

As international research collaborations transcend individual faculty and researcher teams to include global partnerships developed and managed at the institutional level, universities will find it necessary to prioritize relationships and resources. Research projects are a critical avenue to multidimensional partnerships and consortia, which may incorporate expanded opportunities for faculty and students, greater mobility of students and researchers, the articulation of academic degrees and courses (e.g., double or joint degrees, 2+1, 3+2), and the delivery of U.S. degrees to students who never have to leave their home country (Kuder, Lemmens, and Obst 2013). Strategic partnerships are not one-dimensional. They include diverse activities that contribute to research capacity, student learning, and reputation building.

As institutions continue to establish and refine the recipe(s) for successful global research collaborations, institutional leaders and partnership managers must also devise strategies to ensure that the knowledge created by international partnerships contributes to the betterment of society and is effectively communicated outward to those who can put discovery into practice.

References

Arasu, Prema. 2016. "Metrics for Institutional Assessments of the Impact of International Research Collaboration." Poster presented at the AAAS 2016 Annual Meeting, Washington, DC.

Association of Public & Land-grant Universities (APLU) Commission on International Initiatives. 2017. *Pervasive Internationalization: A Call for Renewed Leadership*. Washington, DC: Association of Public & Land-grant Universities. http://www.aplu.org/library/pervasive-internationalization-a-call-for-renewed-leadership/file.

Banks, Clare, Birgit Siebe-Herbig, and Karin Norton, eds. 2016. *Global Perspectives on Strategic International Partnerships: A Guide to Building Sustainable Academic Linkages*. Institute of International Education and German Academic Exchange Service (DAAD).

Brustein, William, and Maureen Miller. 2011. "Using Global Gateway Offices as a Model for Expanding International Partnerships." In *Developing Strategic International Partnerships: Models for Initiating and Sustaining Innovative Institutional Linkages*, eds. Susan Buck Sutton and Daniel Obst. New York, NY: Institute of International Education.

Caruson, Kiki. 2017. *Global Research Toolkit Survey Results 2017*. Tampa, FL: University of South Florida. www.lib.usf.edu/GlobalResearchToolkit.

Colglazier, E. William, and Elizabeth E. Lyons. 2014. "The United States Looks to the Global Science, Technology, and Innovation Horizon." *Science & Diplomacy* 3, 3. Published electronically July 8, 2014. http://www.sciencediplomacy.org/perspective/2014/united-states-looks-global-science-technology-and-innovation-horizon.

Colledge, Lisa. 2017. *Snowball Metrics Recipe Book, 3rd Edition*. The Netherlands: Elsevier. https://www.snowballmetrics.com/wp-content/uploads/0211-Snowball-Metrics-Recipe-Book-v7-LO-1.pdf.

Consultative Group for International Agricultural Research (CGIAR). n.d. "International Rice Research Institute (IRRI)." Montpellier, France: CGIAR. https://www.cgiar.org/research/center/irri.

de Grijs, Richard. 2015. "Ten Simple Rules for Establishing International Research Collaborations." *PLoS Computational Biology* 11, 10:e1004311. https://doi.org/10.1371/journal.pcbi.1004311.

The European Organization for Nuclear Research (CERN). 2018. "About CERN." Switzerland: CERN. https://www.home.cern/about.

Global Research Council. 2017. "Statement of Principles: Capacity Building and Connectivity Among Granting Agencies Worldwide." Global Research Council. https://www.globalresearchcouncil.org/fileadmin/documents/GRC_Publications/Statement_of_Principles_for_Capacity_Building_and_Connectivity_Among_Granting_Agencies_Worldwide.pdf.

Holbrook, Karen A., and Kiki Caruson. 2017. *Globalizing University Research: Innovation, Collaboration, and Competition*. New York, NY: Institute of International Education.

Industrial Research Institute. 2017a. "Academia Continues as Nation's Basic Research Hub." *2017 Global R&D Funding Forecast. R&D Magazine*. Winter 2017. http://digital.rdmag.com/researchanddevelopment/2017_global_r_d_funding_forecast?pg=12#pg12.

Industrial Research Institute. 2017b. "Globalization Changed Everything." *2017 Global R&D Funding Forecast. R&D Magazine*. Winter 2017. http://digital.rdmag.com/researchanddevelopment/2017_global_r_d_funding_forecast?pg=21#pg21.

Kuder, Matthias. 2015. *Current Trends in Strategic Partnerships*. Berlin, Germany: Freie Universität Berlin. https://www2.daad.de/medien/hochschulen/ww/hspartnerschaften/strp/tagung_going_forward_kuder.pdf.

Kuder, Mattias, Nina Lemmens, and Daniel Obst, eds. 2013. *Global Perspectives on International and Joint and Double Degree Programs*. New York, NY: Institute of International Education.

McCarthy, Niall. 2017. "The Most and Least Expensive Countries for Broadband." *Forbes*. November 22, 2017. https://www.forbes.com/sites/niallmccarthy/2017/11/22/the-most-and-least-expensive-countries-for-broadband-infographic/#3da5baee23ef.

Metcalfe, Janet, and Emma Day. 2016. *Equality and Status of Women in Research: Survey Report for the Global Research Council 2016 Annual Meeting.* Careers Research and Advisory Centre (CRAC) Limited. https://www.globalresearchcouncil.org/fileadmin//documents/GRC_Publications/Survey_Report_on_Equality_for_GRC_Vitae.pdf.

National Aeronautics and Space Administration (NASA). 2017. "International Cooperation." Washington, DC: National Aeronautics and Space Administration. https://www.nasa.gov/mission_pages/station/cooperation/index.html.

National Intelligence Council. 2017. *Global Trends: Paradoxes of Progress.* Washington, DC: National Intelligence Council. https://www.dni.gov/files/documents/nic/GT-Full-Report.pdf.

Pain, Elisabeth. 2017. "French President's Climate Talent Search Nabs 18 Foreign Scientists." *Science.* Published electronically December 11, 2017. doi:10.1126/science.aar7290. http://www.sciencemag.org/news/2017/12/french-president-s-climate-talent-search-nabs-18-foreign-scientists.

Plume, Andrew. 2014. "Impact of Science: The Need to Measure." Elsevier Connect. The Netherlands: Elsevier.

Proctor, Douglas. 2016. "Stakeholder Engagement for Successful International Partnerships: Faculty and Staff Roles." In *Global Perspectives on Strategic International Partnerships: A Guide to Building Sustainable Academic Linkages,* eds. Clare Banks, Birgit Siebe-Herbig, and Karin Norton. Institute of International Education and German Academic Exchange Service (DAAD).

Romo, Alvaro. 2015. "Strategic International Partnerships – The Leader's Role." *University World News* 393. December 4, 2015. http://www.universityworldnews.com/article.php?story=20151202151421775.

Romo, Alvaro. 2016. "Strategic International Partnerships: The University Leadership Point of View." In *Global Perspectives on Strategic International Partnerships: A Guide to Building Sustainable Academic Linkages,* eds. Clare Banks, Birgit Siebe-Herbig, and Karin Norton. Institute of International Education and German Academic Exchange Service (DAAD).

Sloan, Susan Sauer, and Joe Alper. 2014. *Culture Matters: International Research Collaboration in a Changing World: Summary of a Workshop.* Washington, DC: National Academy of Sciences.

Sloan, Susan Sauer, and Tom Arrison. 2011. *Examining Core Elements of International Research Collaboration: Summary of Workshop.* Washington, DC: National Academy of Sciences.

Snowball Metrics. n.d. "Snowball Metrics." The Netherlands: Elsevier. https://www.snowballmetrics.com.

United Nations. n.d. "Sustainable Development Goals." United Nations. http://www.un.org/sustainabledevelopment/sustainable-development-goals.

United Nations. 2015. *Transforming Our World: The 2030 Agenda for Sustainable Development*. United Nations. http://www.un.org/ga/search/view_doc.asp?symbol=A/RES/70/1&Lang=E.

University of Exeter. 2017. "Universities of Exeter and Queensland Cement New Global Impact Partnership." Exeter, United Kingdom: University of Exeter. June 2, 2017. https://www.exeter.ac.uk/international/news/international/title_586569_en.html.

West, Charlotte. 2012. *Engaging Stakeholders in Internationalization: Strategies for Collaboration*. Washington, DC: NAFSA: Association of International Educators.

4

Community of Local and International Partnerships to Advance Internationalization

Joël A. Gallegos

The internationalization of a university requires a complex configuration and extensive framework of academic, cocurricular, cultural, and student-centered activities, as well as stakeholder support. This institutional internationalization framework can be greatly strengthened and enhanced through the building of strategic and thoughtful partnerships among the many resources available in the surrounding community, the larger region, and in communities of exchange partners abroad. By forging and cultivating intentional and meaningful local community and international connections, institutions can design innovative and intensified internationalization and global strategies.

To advance institutional goals of internationalization, one must look well beyond the boundaries of the campus; yet in many instances, an institution only utilizes its exchange and university partners abroad for traditional semester and yearlong programming. Too often, institutions overlook or do not fully optimize the robust local and international community resources that provide myriad international education engagement and value-added opportunities for programming, fundraising, and expert input. The tendency to limit the definition of "international partnerships" to include only those connections providing conventional education abroad opportunities to students can compromise the network of potential internationalization mission contributors. The lack of emphasis on community engagement, local and abroad, may be a result of limited capacity or countless competing priorities, yet the benefits may certainly outweigh the challenges associated with developing them. Local communities, as well as those regions of international partnerships, should be equally considered when examining the scope and advantages of possible connections.

This chapter provides considerations and recommendations for establishing effective partnerships for community engagement, as well as examples of potential community partners. It explores how such partnerships may be developed to contribute to the institution's internationalization mission and the work of the international education leader, while also furthering the campus's broader responsibility to deepen its engagement with the local community. Nearly every higher education institution, public or private, large or small, research extensive or teaching, is committed to deepening its bonds with its community and adding value as a local resource, and partnerships are an effective approach to accomplish these charges.

Unique Advantages

No matter the geography or size of an institution, urban or rural, large or small, each has certain unique advantages from which to draw. For senior international officers (SIOs), building on the various community networks affiliated with an institution plays an important role in the work of campus internationalization. Every college and university is associated with various types of communities, so all SIOs have the ability to engage in the development of strategic community partnerships. Whether an international office is the region's primary "international go-to" resource or it is simply one of many local entities with an internationally related mission in the area, one can capitalize on those connections accessible in the local community in addition to those existing in and around international partner locales.

All institutions have many different external community relationships. Senior administrators are often tasked with serving on local community boards, and business schools may have a variety of connections with the area's corporate landscape. Schools of education are often closely connected with local school districts and departments of instruction, engineering programs are associated with industry partners for co-op placements, and medical schools collaborate closely and are allied with area hospitals and health care networks.

University presidents and constituent relations teams often manage complex and sensitive connections with local and elected government officials as well.

These strategic connections may have matured over the course of many years for very specific purposes, but they may not have always been considered for their potential impact on or opportunity for the internationalization of the university. However, the SIO can cultivate an ecosystem of thoughtful and deliberate local and international community partners who can amplify how the institution advances its strategic internationalization goals.

In addition to the campus relationships and partnerships existing within the local community, one must not overlook those international resources and networks affiliated with connections abroad that could also contribute to the institution's global footprint. The local communities in which exchange partner institutions are located can also provide numerous opportunities, ranging from service learning, internships, and short-term programing engagement to faculty research and economic development.

Institutional Culture and Awareness

While the management of the institution's network of international exchange and memorandum of understanding (MOU) partnerships is often configured within the SIO portfolio, the pathway to other forms of partnerships that can advance internationalization, including community engagement, local or abroad, may be less obvious. That said, it is important to be familiar with and understand how an institution values and approaches relationships beyond exchange agreements.

It is commonplace for an institution to engage with its local community in many ways. The SIO, on the other hand, particularly those who are newer to the role, may have fewer existing connections within a local community, but could benefit significantly from this network.

Prior to considering who may be a potential strategic community partner and where there is existing institutional overlap or interest, it is important to begin thinking about institutional culture, primarily its appetite for partnership and how its strategy for community engagement can be complementary to its internationalization goals. No higher education institution functions in precisely the same way, thus the institutional culture often drives how partnerships are developed.

Institutional community connections have often evolved over time, and the most successful ones have involved sustained engagement by campus stakeholders. These individuals have invested time and resources into maintaining those relationships that are beneficial to them, and as such, it is important for the SIO to understand when to capitalize on existing relationships and when to develop new ones. For example, while an institution may have long-standing connections with a local corporation or organization, despite the potential to advance internationalization, these partnerships may be limited to a very defined direction or purpose. It is crucial for the SIO to determine when certain relationships may be off-limits. There may be overarching fundraising plans or other initiatives addressing alternative campus priorities that are tied to the specific parameters of the partnership.

The SIO must have open conversations with campus leadership and other colleagues to build trust and to better address and avoid turf-related issues. This ongoing dialogue could also help build valuable social capital as a result of enhanced collaboration with on-campus partners. The SIO can incorporate topics pertaining to community engagement into regular agendas with senior administrators and faculty, which will invariably result in a confident knowledge base of colleagues' networks, local and abroad. Articulating how these connections may enhance internationalization opportunities may be welcomed and embraced by colleagues because they add innovation and new energy to long-standing connections. It is the role of the SIO to develop compelling rationale for building these networks and to eloquently capture how they can favorably influence internationalization.

Development of an Inventory of Local Connections for Engagement

Most "town and gown" relationships are often intentionally developed, curated, and managed by campus leaders at the highest administrative levels—from the president to vice presidents and deans. These complex interactions often have greater reputational risk involved because they are aligned with overarching and strategic institutional goals for fundraising and corporate sponsorship as well as academic partnership. The far-reaching effects of community relationships often have direct lines of communication with and impact on leadership.

The SIO must seek input from a variety of campus leaders and be familiar with how the institution approaches, manages, and sustains these types of partnerships before beginning to expand the institution's local reach. The SIO should determine the latitude for engaging with existing campus connections and pursuing new ones. Each campus may have very defined protocols (either explicitly articulated or implied) regarding developing community partnerships. Being acutely aware of and sensitized to this process will inform the SIO on how to best navigate the development of the ecosystem of community partners.

In developing a blueprint for a network of community alliances, the SIO need not start from ground zero. Through the existing affiliations with campus leaders, the SIO can begin to engineer discussions regarding their extended networks and how those connections can favorably contribute to internationalization priorities. Campus allies not only provide invaluable insight on how to engage the community from the perspective of the campus culture, but they can also direct the SIO to creative and innovative partners, either existing connections or new ones, and can facilitate introductions with possible partners who would be suitable for advancing internationalization goals.

It may be useful to develop an inventory of current connections within the community as well as the institution's connections that may have overlap or potential alignment with the internationalization goals and interests. Knowing who on campus is doing what, with whom, will be indispensable in formulating and expanding the partnership framework.

Developing this inventory need not necessarily be a formal survey or query, but may be developed through a series of organic discussions with campus leaders and information gleaned from already developed campus resource collateral. Valuable on-campus resource contacts for this exercise may include faculty and staff in the school of business and offices of career services, community engagement, and research.

If it is determined that a brief survey would be the most effective mechanism for compiling this information, then first obtaining the provost's or president's endorsement may encourage more feedback from campus colleagues. A survey could simply collect information on the community partner and primary campus contact; yet, more detailed information may be insightful, such as when the relationship began, examples of joint initiatives, whether the relationship is considered successful, and whether or not the campus contact would be interested in introducing the SIO as a new campus partner. Regardless, the survey should be presented as a way to collectively strengthen and add value to the campus's internationalization reach. As already mentioned, many campus colleagues may not have given extensive thought as to how their connections in the community could advance internationalization goals.

In developing a more detailed and thorough understanding of how specific relationships are brokered and managed, the SIO can begin to determine if, how, and where to best gain access to that network. Both universities and local communities are highly complex entities, and identifying areas of cooperation and mutuality may seem overwhelming, but developing a defined plan will ease the challenge. Through incorporating an international dimension into local community engagement and partnerships, existing connections can be fortified in new and innovative ways.

Community Engagement Connections Abroad

While most institutions have long had extensive university-to-university partnerships abroad for semester and yearlong faculty and student exchanges, they may be less likely to have community engagement contacts within those cities or regions in which these exchange agreements are located. Whether or not an institution has already formulated connections in those communities, the SIO can strategize on how these possible partners could contribute to the institution's internationalization goals.

For instance, exchange partners typically have connections with their local research and development parks. To that end, there may be faculty members on the SIO's campus with research interests that are aligned with those potential research connections abroad. It could be useful for the SIO to investigate those possible areas of mutuality and share them with the vice presidents for research and other senior academic administrators. This alignment could result in further strengthening the connection between the home and partner institutions. While the outcome is rarely predictable when attempting to connect faculty members with possible research collaborators, fostering these opportunities of introduction could be highly appreciated.

From the perspective of economic development initiatives, many campuses now host university-industry partnership hubs. These centers on campus are often responsible for promoting research and innovation while accelerating business opportunities for the university region. Faculty and staff in these centers are well positioned to consider creative and entrepreneurial connections at home and abroad. Introducing these individuals to colleagues overseas could result in new programming in research and business development opportunities between the two regions.

With regard to student programming, there could be various nongovernmental organizations and other nonprofit organizations in those locales abroad from which to draw service-learning and internship programs for students. Faculty members who are interested in developing such programs may welcome an introduction to new partners who can provide students with meaningful community engagement and professional learning and work experiences overseas. Local art communities and museums may also be replete with opportunities for collaboration. Local theaters, orchestras, and artist cooperatives could likewise be potential community partners abroad. These connections could enhance the institution's student programming and faculty research and contribute to a pool of international guest speakers and visiting experts on campus.

These are just a few examples of possible community connections that the SIO can engage to enhance institutional connectedness abroad. Depending on the size and complexities of these communities overseas, there could be countless other community assets who are willing to serve as partners to expand the institution's network of programming engagement.

Ecosystem of Potential Community Partners

Given that so many institutions highlight their commitment to and connection with their surrounding community and beyond, there is prime opportunity for international educators to develop their own sub-ecosystem of engagement. It would be advantageous for the SIO to step back and reflect on how the internationalization of the campus is, or might be, interconnected to a wide variety of community organizations and individuals, locally and abroad. While the value-added quotient of each relationship or connection may not be uniform, many will provide new perspectives, potential avenues for fundraising, and dialogue to increase the international office's operational visibility and social capital.

Depending on one's region or city and where the institution engages abroad, the number of potential community partners could be quite significant. As such, it is important to consider the SIO's capacity for cultivating these connections and to prioritize how they relate to the institution's mission before identifying those individuals or entities with a commitment to or interest in international and global affairs. While budget and time limitations, along with competing priorities, are important when considering the extended network, the value of these community engagement partnerships must not be underestimated.

Potential Partners

This section highlights some local, regional, and international entities that could potentially be featured in the international education sub-ecosystem (see figure 1). Each entity listed below can provide a number of opportunities and benefits to the internationalization of a campus. In addition to offering advice and guidance on international and global affairs, these partners can enhance the SIO's profile by promoting and educating others on the institution's commitment to international education. The more familiar that these potential partners are with the mission and objectives related to international education, the better positioned they are to support the work of the SIO. One should not assume that off-campus individuals and organizations grasp the complexities of an SIO portfolio; therefore, the opportunity to inform these potential community partners of the breadth and scope of international education programming and engagement could be mutually advantageous.

Some of the potential benefits of collaborating with community partners include increasing visibility, expanding networks, identifying new avenues for

Figure 1. Ecosystem of Potential Community Partners

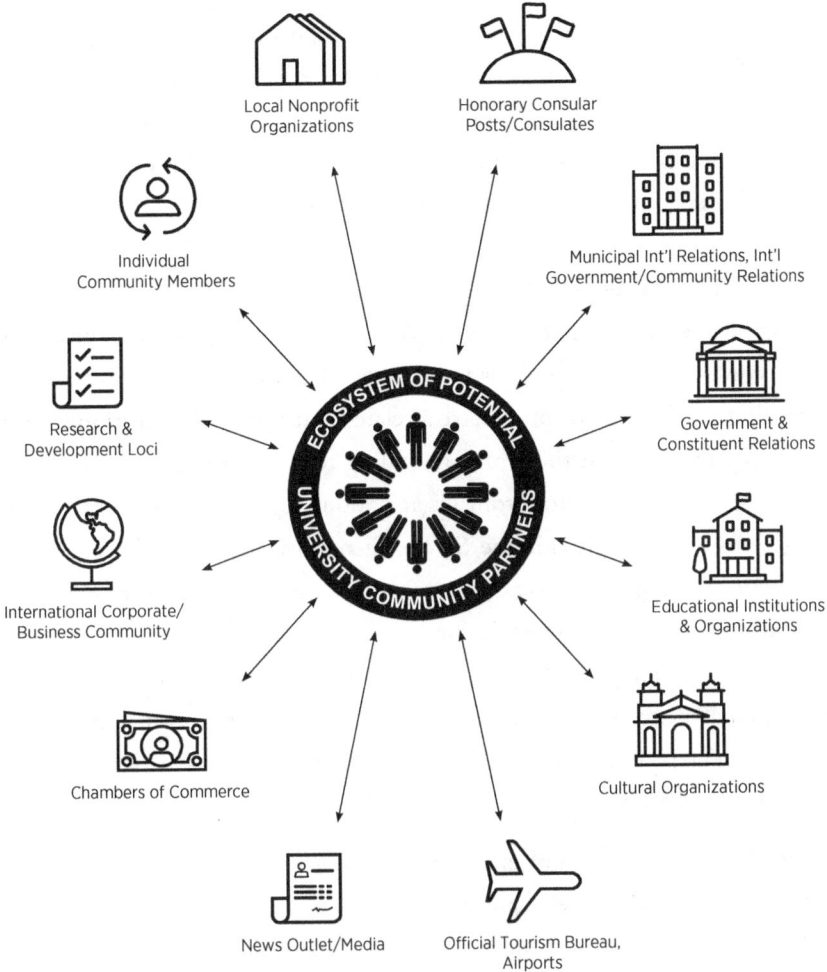

Local Nonprofit
Organizations

Honorary Consular
Posts/Consulates

Municipal Int'l Relations, Int'l
Government/Community Relations

Individual
Community Members

Government &
Constituent Relations

Research &
Development Loci

Educational Institutions
& Organizations

International Corporate/
Business Community

Cultural Organizations

Chambers of Commerce

News Outlet/Media

Official Tourism Bureau,
Airports

DESIGNED BY: ELOI SOLIS & ALAYNA GOROSPE

fundraising and programming, and developing internship and experiential learning opportunities for students. While the drawbacks are few, it is important to understand that as one cultivates these partnerships, it does take effort, planning, and enthusiasm. The ability of the SIO to navigate and balance these community partners, in addition to core responsibilities on campus, is important to consider. Setting reasonable goals of expanding one's network by one or two community partners per semester could be a practical approach to establishing this sub-ecosystem. Attempting to juggle too many newly developed partnerships too quickly may require more planning, meetings, and follow-up than one anticipates, so be prepared for some time commitment.

The following are examples of local, regional, and international partners. While the list of potential partnerships is not exhaustive, this community of practitioners will provide a strong starting point.

LOCAL NONPROFIT ORGANIZATIONS

Among all the potential community partners, local nonprofit organizations may serve as the most logical place to start and can be rich resources as programming partners. They often have a related international education or soft diplomacy mission and therefore are willing to forge stronger relationships with local institutions. Nonprofit organizations regularly host international delegations and can provide the SIO with opportunities to cohost visitors and cosponsor expert speakers. However, it is important to note that some nonprofit organizations are underfunded and understaffed, so their financial resources may be limited. Yet they are regularly aligned with the university's international office mission and offer great value and connections. Some examples of local nonprofit organizations include Sister Cities International, World Affairs Council Chapters, and International Houses.

Sister Cities International encourages citizen diplomacy through educational, cultural, and civic exchanges. Many communities develop institutional exchange partners with institutions in sister cities. If this practice of exchange partner development does not currently exist, it is recommended that the SIO first consider institutional alignment rather than simply assuming those institutions located in sister cities are a strategic fit for the exchange partner network. Local Sister Cities Committees are often comprised of committed and enthusiastic community members who could also be helpful to the SIO.

World Affairs Council Chapters across the United States offer programs and educational initiatives to institutions, conferences, and town halls that spark discourse around foreign policy and the United States's role in the international arena. These chapters often host prominent speakers and global thought leaders and can collaborate with the institution on campus and community events. They may also have deep connections in the corporate community that could provide the SIO entrée into new networks of potential stakeholders.

International Houses coordinate international visitor programming and local international community festivals. They often have strong ties to international community members in the region. International Houses may also serve as a resource for cultural engagement and programming for international students and scholars.

HONORARY CONSULAR POSTS/CONSULATES

These official representatives can facilitate trade and cultural connections and are great resources when the SIO is traveling or cultivating partnerships abroad. The SIO may want to connect with the consulates for information on potential diplomatic speakers.

MUNICIPAL INTERNATIONAL RELATIONS

City Protocol is often the area that city officials rely on for engagement with foreign visitors, dignitaries, and other official international visitors. Staff can provide the SIO with valuable introductions to new exchange partners and other networks abroad.

The Office of International Relations offers resources to help foster international partnerships and connections to a city or region as well as to local international communities. Staff can share best practices for coordinating international delegations. While this office may not exist in each community, if available, it can be a strategic partner to the SIO.

GOVERNMENT AND CONSTITUENT RELATIONS

Government officials can offer nonpartisan international student and scholar advocacy support, but it is critical to connect with any institutional constituent relations team prior to developing a partnership.

EDUCATIONAL INSTITUTIONS AND ORGANIZATIONS

In addition to other higher education institutions and those in the K–12 school system in one's area or abroad, there are other communities of educators with whom to partner, collaborate, and dialogue. Libraries can serve as a strong partner in developing international book fairs, hosting visiting authors, and promoting other internationally related literacy projects.

CULTURAL ORGANIZATIONS

Museums, orchestras, symphonies, performing arts centers, and cinemas provide numerous opportunities to team up on global programming and cobranding for heightened visibility of events. For example, institutions can partner on international performances or international film festivals to engage the wider community and advance internationalize efforts more broadly.

OFFICIAL TOURISM BUREAU AND AIRPORTS

Given the potential overlap in international travel-related functions, the official tourism bureau and area airports can serve as informational resources regarding new international travel and flight initiatives, local airline updates, and tourism material for incoming delegations and students.

NEWS OUTLETS AND THE MEDIA

Thoughtful and strategic communications and interviews through the local media channels, including television, radio, newspapers, local magazines, and other periodicals, can assist in amplifying an institution's international education commitment. Depending on how the institutional communications are managed, the SIO may have the chance to promote the events and programs on campus. In those cases, the SIO will want to work with the institution's communications team to make sure that the messaging is in line with the institution's official voice, position, and branding.

Conversely, it may be advantageous for the SIO to develop a connection with respected news officials in the area so that when a story about international students or education abroad breaks, the SIO may be the first one to be contacted for a response. Additionally, when the media is seeking expert opinions and resources on in-depth articles, the SIO may be called on to offer a quote or full interview, further positioning the institution as a leader in the field.

CHAMBERS OF COMMERCE

Some institutions may choose to engage in the corporate and business networks focused on strengthening trade and industry. Such partners may include the local Chamber of Commerce as well as specific internationally focused chambers of commerce such as the Asian American Chamber of Commerce, Franco-American Chamber of Commerce, and Latin American Chamber of Commerce. These groups can provide institutions, and their students, access to local cultural and business communities that support internationalization.

INTERNATIONAL CORPORATE AND BUSINESS COMMUNITY

Taking a wider outlook, some SIOs form mutually beneficial links with the international corporate and business community, including those organizations that have offices, branches, or even headquarters in the local area but have a global reach. These potential partners can be critical in networking and fundraising interests. They can also draw from local experts for international speakers and serve as hosts for student internships abroad.

RESEARCH AND DEVELOPMENT LOCI

Often a hotbed of significant international engagement, research and development parks often host international scholars and scientists or may collaborate on research projects abroad. Institutional research officials are usually already connected to these individuals and may have relevant contacts for the SIO.

INDIVIDUAL COMMUNITY MEMBERS

There are numerous individuals within the community with whom the SIO and institution can establish a productive partnership to advance initiatives. These may include individual donors, immigration experts, local content experts, economists, artists, and authors. The SIO may reach out to staff from local ethnic restaurants and travel agents as possible individual partners as well. Each partner can offer a different perspective, network of contacts, and contribution that enhances or augments the institution's internationalization agenda.

Benefits of Community Partnerships

The results from creating a robust network of community partners who share in the goal of advancing internationalization of the institution can yield significant benefits. These partnerships can provide rich resources that complement an existing portfolio or innovate international engagement programs that have not yet been developed. Below are various domains that can be supported through the development of community partnerships.

- Experiential learning opportunities for students. Whether through the variety of nonprofit international organizations in the area, within local companies, or with entities abroad, one's community connections may yield experiential learning opportunities in the community and abroad. Many local industries rely on local higher education institutions to provide skills training to their workforce. These companies could collaborate with the institution on internships and other experiential opportunities either in local businesses or with their foreign-based subsidiaries.

- Cultural programming. Different partners in the community are often quite eager to mobilize and collaborate on various types of cultural programs. These programs may involve opportunities for students, faculty, and staff, but they also could engage the community members at large. Events and activities could include international cultural festivals, international film series, international holiday fairs, and community lecture series.

- Fundraising. Many institutions have a sophisticated infrastructure for identifying potential prospects for the purposes of fundraising. While campus fundraisers have guided priorities set by senior administration and deans, formulating opportunities that include the international office could be advantageous. To that end, the interface with community partners can provide international educators with a network that may be strategically developed in collaboration with the institutional advancement office. This on-campus partnership, in conjunction with intentionally identified community members, may result in scholarship funds for education abroad or incoming international students. Furthermore, named or endowed signature international education initiatives could be compelling initiatives that community members may potentially support.

- Potential grant partners. Many internationally related grant and funding opportunities include the development of partnerships within the community. Having an established network of local schools and corporate connections at the ready could provide for a quick grant submission turnaround. When submitting a grant proposal, this existing framework of connections is highly desirable given the short deadlines for submission.

- Heightened visibility. The SIO can take advantage of connections with various media outlets and other entities with influential community reach to better amplify and promote the institution's mission and goals within and to the community. For example, this may include the development of a partnership with the local protocol office in hosting a high-level international delegation and promoting International Education Week or festivals in the local newspaper or evening news.

- Local and international expertise. In the process of expanding the institution's community network, the international office may start to build a list of invaluable resources to serve as content experts. These individuals can include immigration experts, local documentarians and authors, prominent researchers, philanthropists, and entrepreneurs. Depending on the nature and scope of the institution's international education programming portfolio, this could be a very rich pool from which to identify possible speakers, develop programs in partnership, or serve on an internationally related advisory council or board on campus.

Challenges, Obstacles, and Pitfalls of Community Partnerships

While the benefits of successful strategic community engagement can certainly outweigh the challenges, one must consider possible obstacles and pitfalls. One challenge that international educators are likely to experience from time to time when engaging with local networks is the perception of infringing on someone's already existing partnership or resource contact. This type of overlap may be more common among institutional colleagues and stakeholders. Or, the university may be competing with other institutions vying for the same connections or limited resources available. The opportunity cost involved might result in strained connections or misunderstandings that will require address. Again, a willingness to engage in open conversations regarding community engagement to advance internationalization with on-campus partners can be invaluable when navigating these dynamics.

When developing connections within the local framework, it is always advisable to approach new relationships from an information gathering point of view. By doing so—even if the SIO is unable to glean an existing relationship from other campus resources or colleagues—it may reveal how the various community entities and organizations interact with the campus. With that knowledge in hand, the SIO can better identify how to align priorities and interests and determine complementarity.

The development of an on-campus community engagement inventory can assist in avoiding overstepping and minimizing redundancy. It is important to note that the process involved in creating such an inventory will take time and may occur incrementally. In general, institutions tend to function in silos and it is often difficult to collect information, formally or informally. If there is top-down support for the development of a more proactive community engagement plan, then a more formal survey might be an avenue to pursue. If, on the other hand, this is an initiative that the SIO would like to begin from a grassroots level on campus, having ongoing discussions with colleagues may be the most effective approach.

The failure to identify and articulate how the partnership is mutually beneficial is also a potential pitfall. When developing any partnership, it is important for both partners to clearly understand why one would enter into any collaboration. Keep in mind that for an ecosystem to function successfully, all parties must achieve some level of benefit from the interaction. As a whole, international educators are committed to advancing global awareness and learning, yet not all community members are potentially aligned and sensitized to this mission. To the extent possible, understanding the full complement of resources that exist in the community will better prepare the SIO to determine and select those that should be emphasized.

Additionally, it is extremely important to recognize the effort required to develop, cultivate, and sustain community relationships. It takes planning and thoughtful consideration to identify strategies that assist in advancing campus internationalization while avoiding reputational risk. To that end, it is critical to understand the capacity the SIO and international office have for developing these kinds of partnerships. Obviously, such partnership development and sustainability should not be approached as a solo mission, but if the SIO is to serve as the principal or driver of the engagement, it is important to understand how much time, effort, and resources it will draw from one's current focus and existing portfolio. For example, the SIO may determine at first that only a minimal level of engagement is possible as the partnership framework is being developed, and, over the course of 1 or 2 years, a new opportunity or connection is added each term. After a few years, the SIO may have established a core group of community partners and a blueprint for optimizing these relationships.

Exemplars of Community Engagement for Internationalization

There are countless ways in which an institution can engage with its community to advance internationalization. These types of initiatives can involve community cultural programs, educational opportunities, and fundraising for education abroad scholarships. While there is not one single blueprint to develop such connections, the following are successful examples of community partnerships that have evolved over time and have greatly enhanced internationalization on campus and in the surrounding community:

The **Collaborative Theater Initiative** is an innovative and unique experiential education abroad program in London, England, that stems from a partnership between the University of Minnesota and the internationally recognized Guthrie Theatre. The program supports student development in actor training and myriad other dimensions of performance and culminates in a production of Shakespeare at the Globe Theatre, also located in London. The curriculum is developed jointly between the University of Minnesota and Guthrie Theatre, and the partners also collaborate to raise scholarship funds.

German Language and Culture Foundation (GLCF) of Charlotte aims to provide education abroad scholarships to students in Charlotte, North Carolina, while promoting Germany throughout the greater metropolitan area. Given Charlotte's concentration of German-based companies (209) (see Wilson 2018), there is a need to graduate area students who have a level of German language proficiency and an awareness of and interest in the German culture. While the GLCF raises funds for many educational initiatives (e.g., speakers, cultural events, and festivals) in the local community, most of the funding goes to university students. Since 2010, the GLCF has awarded more than $500,000 in scholarships to 246 students at the University of North Carolina at Charlotte (UNC Charlotte) to study in Germany.

This renaissance of interest in German language and culture revived a language program that now graduates 43 German majors annually, making it the second highest enrolled German language program in the United States (The Chronicle List 2019). The increase in German majors has been significant. In 2010, there were 32 enrolled students majoring in German, and in 2019, there were 120 majors. Much of this enthusiasm has been borne out of the ability to send a high number of students to Germany with sponsored scholarship funding.

Many of the German companies based in Charlotte are committed to annual fundraising events and corporate sponsorship, which allows them to both provide back to the community and address their need for a more prepared workforce. Indeed, these companies have the opportunity to develop soft recruiting strategies for their employment needs while positively impacting university students. In addition, the companies often provide experiential work placements following the students' education abroad experiences.

Great Decision Lecture Series is a national program of the Foreign Policy Association. UNC Charlotte coordinates an annual community lecture series focused on relevant and timely topics and challenges facing the world. The series provides attendees with an opportunity to hear from and discuss world affairs with local experts. While the lecture series often draws more individuals from the community than university students, the attendance composition varies. The lecture series has been ongoing for more than 30 years and offers a consistent outlet for community members to engage with university professors on global topics. It provides an opportunity to increase visibility of the scholars as well as the scope of the institution's expertise on issues related to global affairs.

The annual **International Festival**, coordinated by UNC Charlotte's Office of International Programs, has served as the institution's most visible community event for the last 43 years. Hosting upwards of 20,000 attendees annually (including more than 6,000 university students), the festival is a large-scale celebration featuring cultural representation, performances, food, and educational activities. The event requires significant cooperation between the local international communities, international students and faculty, and campus facilities. There are activities that bring K–12 community schools, teachers, students, and parents to the daylong festival as well.

The **Lifelong Learning Travel Program** highlights the scope of professors' international scholarship. UNC Charlotte created the Green and Gold Travelers Society program over a decade ago, in which the university chancellor, an expert faculty member, and a group of community members travel together to various destinations, focusing on an international topic. The faculty member provides lectures on a daily basis along with relevant visits to cultural sites. If an exchange or education abroad program is also in the area, a visit to meet with the students or institutional partners is included. The initiative began as a way to showcase faculty members' engagement abroad but quickly became an mechanism to educate the community on how the institution engages abroad and has helped to cultivate potential institutional supporters, friends, and donors.

World Affairs Council of Charlotte (WACC) was established in 1983 as an intentional community engagement initiative of the Office of International Programs at UNC Charlotte. WACC's primary mission is to foster dialogue and discourse on global thinking in the local area to better equip community members for effective competition in the global economy, as well as develop responsible citizenship in an increasingly diverse world. WACC's influence spans a broad scope, from K–12 educators through to the local corporate and executive environment. Among its signature programs, WACC coordinates a Council Scholars Program that provides summer education abroad scholarships to local K–12 teachers and counselors on an annual basis. These individuals then commit to increasing global content and awareness in their classrooms.

WACC also founded and coordinates Academic World Quest, which is an internationally focused trivia competition among area high schools (an initiative that has now become a national model among World Affairs Councils). WACC also established a speaker series of prominent individuals who present on topics related to foreign relations and international policy.

While it became an independent 501(c)(3) in 2003, WACC is still housed in the Office of International Programs on UNC Charlotte's campus. The university remains dedicated to its symbiotic relationship with the Council to further its commitment for community engagement. The university draws from WACC's pool of speakers from a variety of backgrounds at no additional cost. The speakers range from current and former national and international ambassadors, well-known economists, business leaders, and authors. These speakers have become the backbone of the Office of International Programs's International Speaker Series, which is held on campus on an annual basis. This series is one of the office's primary and most highly visible on-campus initiatives, with significant student, faculty, and staff attendance at each of its events. Given WACC's connection with the local corporate community and the Chamber of Commerce, it also provides the campus's international office with opportunities to access and interface with business leaders and other prominent officials specifically on topics related to international affairs and global thinking.

Conclusion

The pathway to forging a successful community engagement and partner ecosystem is not always uniform. Developing a clear understanding of the potential value-added impact that community partners can contribute may be the first step in the journey. Once the SIO is able to determine who may potentially be a part of the ecosystem, and why, a framework can be created that is in alignment with the campus culture.

During the development of the campus community engagement inventory, patterns and areas of opportunity may arise. Discussions with campus colleagues may provide greater insight into which partners will be shared and those that may be off-limits. Upon initiating the plan and making new contacts, there will invariably be new opportunities for cooperation and program innovations.

While some partnerships may not provide equal value in the way they were initially envisioned, or certain area contacts may end up lacking the needed commitment, generally, the overall outcomes of the community partnership framework will no doubt add complementary benefits to the institution's internationalization strategies.

References

The Chronicle List. 2019. "Which Colleges Grant the Most Bachelor's Degrees in Foreign Languages." *Chronicle of Higher Education.* January 29, 2019. https://www.chronicle.com/article/Which-Colleges-Grant-the-Most/245567.

Wilson, Jen. 2018. "Inside the Book of Lists: Your Guide to Charlotte's Top Employers, Neighborhoods and More." *Charlotte Business Journal.* December 21, 2018. https://www.bizjournals.com/charlotte/news/2018/12/21/inside-the-book-of-lists-your-guide-to-charlottes.html.

Comprehensive International Partnerships

Jane Gatewood

As the need for higher education increases globally and as research challenges grow in worldwide scope and impact, international partnerships between higher education institutions have become more focused and strategic. Increasingly, partnerships serve as ballast underpinning institutional strategies for international education and global engagement. And concurrently, institutions are rethinking their partnership engagement practices, focusing on impact and outcomes rather than sheer numbers, as has so often been the case.

Jane Knight (2015, pp. 14–15) writes about international institutional agreements in "Five Myths About Internationalization," asserting that "practice shows that most institutions cannot manage or even benefit from a hundred plus agreements. To maintain active and fruitful relationships requires a major investment of human and financial resources from individual faculty members, departments, and international offices." Thus, rather than advocating for the cultivation of myriad agreements, this publication affirms the view that smaller numbers of active, well-curated, and well-stewarded relationships will serve institutions far better than hundreds of agreements on paper only.

Partnerships allow for the combining of complementary resources and intellectual capital for the mutual benefit of all parties, and enable institutions to expand and extend in ways they would not otherwise be capable. In order to leverage their resources most effectively and efficiently, institutions must be deliberate in their partnership development by identifying an international partnership development strategy to cultivate complementary and comprehensive institutional partnerships that align with their own strengths in research, teaching, and service. An external engagement strategy that includes deliberate international partnerships must be underpinned by an institution's own strategy and priorities to be successful. Partnerships that align with institutional strategies and needs will be well positioned to improve an institution's global connections, the cultural awareness and understanding of its students and faculty, and its academic and research impact. This chapter examines approaches to catalyzing, stewarding, and enabling comprehensive partnership development at the institutional level; institutional governance and organizational models; and the importance of trust and familiarity in partnership development.

Comprehensive Partnerships

Various surveys of the international education field chart a steady increase in the role of international partnerships in institutional internationalization (see American Council on Education 2012; Helms and Brajkovic 2017; Marinoni 2019; Sandström and Weimer 2016), and recent iterations have begun to refer to "strategic partnerships." For instance, the *EAIE Barometer* describes international strategic partnerships as "those that encourage durable collaboration…by building sustainable academic networks" and strengthen mobility and knowledge exchanges (Sandström and Weimer 2016, 5). The term "strategic," when used to define one set of institutional relationships as distinct from others, may cast an unintended negative light on those relationships that do not benefit from the moniker. Thus, institutions should approach the use of this and similar terms with some caution. For this reason, this chapter introduces the term "comprehensive partnerships" to mean those cultivated for the long term across multiple disciplines and modes of engagement in line with an institution's broad strategic directions, ethos, and mission.

Comprehensive partnerships are productive and deep multidisciplinary collaborations that expand beyond the initial disciplinary projects and individuals who catalyzed them. Being multifaceted and having disciplinary breadth and programmatic depths that often span multiple units or schools on a given campus, comprehensive international partnerships allow the partner institutions to develop strong institutional ties globally. Additionally, since these relationships are deliberately constructed and curated for the long term, they typically become "generative," producing new opportunities for collaborative engagement as the partner institutions' knowledge of one another deepens (Gatewood and Sutton 2016, 19). Comprehensive partnerships often involve the sharing of resources, research, and curriculum between partners, and they require sustained regular communication as well as financial and staff support. To this end, comprehensive partnerships are most successful when both parties have made institutional commitments in terms of financial and human resources. Also, as relationships cultivated for the long term, comprehensive partnerships involve an intersection of trust and familiarity, with an increase in one area directly increasing that of the other.

Framed and supported appropriately, comprehensive partnerships allow institutions to further their academic reach and extend their research and service impact while also improving each institution's global connections and profile. But equally, individual institutions need to decide what constitutes "comprehensive" in their respective contexts, as well as what types of activities are most appropriate and valuable. For example, smaller, teaching-focused schools may define a comprehensive partnership as one that involves two or three programs developed in concert with an international partner, such as a collaborative degree and student and faculty exchanges with the same institution abroad. Larger, research-intensive institutions, on the other hand, will likely describe comprehensive partnerships in different terms that include research priorities in addition to those related to teaching, learning, and service. No matter the institution type, the priorities for comprehensive partnerships should be rooted firmly in the institutional mission and vision.

Development of Comprehensive Partnerships

Many of the initial questions that arise regarding an institution's international partnership strategy are oriented toward geographic concerns: Where should the institution be engaged? Where should linkages be established? Where is the institution already connected? Where do alumni of the institution live? Where do students study abroad? Where do faculty conduct research? These are, of course, obvious questions related to international activity, whose fulcrum is necessarily geographic. But to know where to go and what to develop, an institution must first discern where it is active internationally, with which partners, and in what types of activities. Such work necessitates a look inward as well as outward, for international engagement informs and engages the home campus as well as its overseas connections.

A look inward, like any self-evaluation, can be filled with uncomfortable truths and realizations, but is necessary for any thoughtful and sustainable growth to occur. So, to know where to go, an institution must first understand where it has been and what it has been doing. These are simple questions to ask, but the answers are often vexing because international activity across campus often remains untracked in various annual reporting measures, embedded in other activities, or comprised of ad hoc and bespoke initiatives that are thought to be outside of traditional on-campus activities.

Uncovering these activities, though, and establishing or revising processes that not only track them but also support and develop them gets at the core of what has been termed "comprehensive internationalization." This process of discovery and recovery often requires retooling institutional processes, and it reveals core international activities, stakeholders, and partners both on and off campus. Such tactics are increasingly critical to the successful identification of comprehensive and sustainable international partners.

Identifying and Enabling Existing Connections

Institutions of all scopes and sizes often have various existing connections that can be ripe candidates for comprehensive collaboration. These partnership opportunities may appear as a constellation of individual activities with the same partner institution abroad, and these individual activities may operate using discrete, vertical channels within the institution. But institutions can develop these disparate connections into a comprehensive relationship by first bringing cohesion to the variety of connections.

A vertical relationship will typically be comprised of faculty-to-faculty or department-to-department engagement. Faculty-to-faculty engagement may include a variety of activities, such as coteaching or coadvising, joint publications, and research, whereas department-to-department activities may expand to include mobility exchanges for students and faculty, joint grant submissions, and collaborative degrees.

Extending horizontally across the organization, comprehensive partnerships will usually have many of the attributes of a vertical relationship, but different vertical elements can be combined into a more robust relationship with various nodes activated in parallel across the organization. As these nodes become more visible, international administrators can work to draw out combined strengths as well as remove other institutional roadblocks to collaboration, so that the broader relationship can be realized and prosper.

To develop internal coherence among a variety of distinct activities, partnership managers need to undertake institutional research, scouring various sources and talking with key stakeholders involved in the existing activities in order to draw out the key thematic areas and activities underpinning the relationship. Internal information sources and types may include annual reports of schools and departments, faculty activity reporting, internationally coauthored publications, subawards for grants, international contracts and agreements, feeder institutions for graduate programs, and sending or receiving institutions for study abroad activities. To help understand the breadth of the institution's global connections, partnership managers may also find it useful to know the locations of alumni living abroad, details regarding patents licensed as well as any other corporate engagement abroad, the degree-granting institutions of faculty members and postdoctoral researchers, and the citizenship and nationality of the institution's students and faculty. By aggregating these various informational resources, institutions can begin to realize patterns as well as gaps in their international connections.

Based on this information gathering and analysis, institutions will likely realize they already have a number of strong partnerships, as well as discover latent links with other partner institutions throughout the world. Once these connections are identified, they can be measured against the institution's own strategic goals. The relationships that align most effectively with institutional strategic priorities should get the most attention from institutional leadership and administration. For these relationships, then, thematic areas of focus and opportunities for future development can be articulated. The development of these areas of focus and opportunity should be undertaken with faculty members, department chairs, and deans who are already engaged in these relationships. Administrators of international partnerships should take considerable care to listen to faculty members' ideas and their real or perceived roadblocks to more engagement. Partnerships rooted in faculty interest, with departmental or disciplinary champions, will develop more organically and richly than those rooted primarily in central leadership's ideas. Although to be clear, partnerships will need support from central leadership to be successful.

Partnership administrators in the international office need to work to ensure an enabling campus environment and administrative infrastructure for the cultivation of comprehensive relationships. Strong communications about successful projects and programs stemming from a partnership will help to grow awareness and cultivate new engagement with the existing partner. These relationships can be furthered through incentives for engagement in the form of faculty reward structures, small grants for travel and seeding new projects, and campus awards for institutional partnerships. Developing an institutional culture that is responsive to partnerships involves a variety of activities, including organizing and supporting periodic high-level partner meetings to discuss and review the constellation of activities ongoing between the partners; occasional internal meetings of campus stakeholders to ensure and promote campus cohesion, share successes, and generate new ideas; and targeted seed grants or supported mobility meetings between the partners to spawn future connections.

Catalyzing New Priority Connections

Occasionally, new institutional relationships will need to be developed where connections are desired but do not currently exist. Various means of making initial connections range from high-level introductory visits to establishing connections via alumni or other trusted intermediaries. The best mode will depend, in part, on the culture of each institution—whether it organizes itself for decisionmaking in a top-down or bottom-up fashion and how receptive it is to overtures from the outside. Prior to outreach, though, institutions should invest some time in researching appropriate partners.

When deciding which institutions to approach for engagement, international offices should review student and faculty interest areas in academics and research abroad and then correlate these with the institution's own strategic research and academic priorities. Doing this will help to refine the list of possible partners.

For instance, if students continually express an interest in studying in a specific region and faculty annual reports highlight extant research collaborations and coauthorships in several countries in the same region, then international office staff can review those institutions with which faculty already have connections. The international institutions that align best with the home institution's needs and strategic priorities can be placed on a short list for possible collaboration. From this list, international offices can make contact and arrange for initial discussions either in person at various conferences or virtually.

Beyond the initial connections, though, partnership managers need to utilize various tactics to catalyze comprehensive connections. Partnerships that foster robust engagement by faculty members will often grow deep and durable roots, and for this reason, mechanisms that include faculty members in partnership development often are the most successful. Strategies that foster faculty engagement, such as collaborative workshops and short-term visits for lectures and seminars, yield effective results in both the initial engagement and periodic re-engagement of partners.

Collaborative workshops for faculty can serve to introduce faculty members from each of the partner institutions to one another. These workshops typically occur over the span of a few days or a week as a select group of faculty members travel from one partner institution to the other as a cohort, staffed by members of the international office. Over the course of the visit, the guests are introduced to the partner institution's faculty members, facilities, laboratories, and students, while the host institution is able to learn more about the guests' research and academic strengths via workshops on topics that have been mutually agreed upon in advance. Faculty members often present on their research and academic areas of strength, which are likely to be topics of common interest between the partners, and international office staff provide overviews of the institutions. International office staff also provide administrative support for the faculty-to-faculty workshops, facilitating discussion, taking notes, and writing summary reports of key topical areas of interest and possible modes of engagement. These summaries help to identify areas of complementarity ripe for collaboration between the institutions. At each stage of connection, partnership managers should develop a practice of keeping notes, ideally in a centralized database or other relationship management tool, including the meeting participants, discussion points, outcomes, and next steps.

Partnership managers at each institution should plan for time to debrief with their faculty members, listening to areas of interest as well as areas of concern. Subsequently, partnership managers from both institutions should connect to discuss and implement a plan for engagement. In these collaborative discussions, partnership managers should triage opportunities for engagement, ranking them from easiest to enact to most complex, and identify those that have strong faculty champions. Institutional partnership managers will want to attend to the financial needs of each modality, identifying those activities that can be self-funding (e.g., reciprocal student exchanges), those that may be suitable for external grant funding (e.g., collaborative research projects), and those that will need more internal or external support for success (e.g., scholarly and faculty exchanges). At this point, discussions with leadership will help to prioritize the identified areas for collaboration.

To move beyond these initial points of connection, partnership managers need to maintain momentum by implementing any agreements that can facilitate the collaboration—such as agreements for student exchange or memoranda of understanding to help support external grant applications—and by developing action plans for all anticipated collaborative activities. Periodic contact with the partner, either through occasional visits or electronic communication, will strengthen the relationship and establish a regularized structure for engagement and information sharing.

Ideally, partnership development will involve a combination of senior leadership and faculty engagement. Senior leaders can open doors that partnership managers and faculty cannot, while robust faculty engagement will serve as the core of the relationship. For a partnership to grow successfully, all levels of the institution need to be involved: senior leadership for strategy and support, faculty members and students for the fundamental activities that comprise the relationship, and international office staff for administration and support of the relationship.

Figure 1 illustrates the stages of partnership development, from partner identification to continuous improvement. Agreement-only relationships typically start in the middle of this development cycle, at the formalization stage, leaping over critical phases of identification and selection, which involve important aspects of internal review and external calibration with the potential partner. These initial stages serve to establish firm internal focus and strong external connections that are the core ballast for relationship development and should not be overlooked.

Figure 1. Stages of Partnership Development

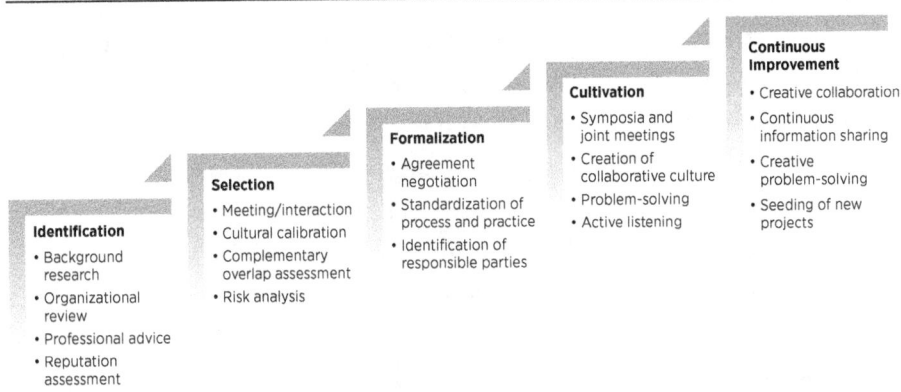

Organizational Culture and Trust Dynamics

Barbara Sporn (1996) categorizes different types of organizational cultures as being oriented either internally or externally (internal versus external) and as having either "strong" or "weak" governance structures, depending on the institution's tendency toward centralization. Sporn (1996, 47) asserts that "if the culture is more internally focused and has decentralized characteristics, the mission as well as the intentions will concentrate on internal effectiveness and autonomy of departments." In such an internally focused environment, strategy development and strategic planning effectiveness can be limited. Equally, in heavily decentralized environments that are also oriented more internally than externally, cohesive international engagement and comprehensive institutional partnerships can be more difficult to develop and steward.

Institutional culture and internal relationships factor considerably when institutions desire to develop comprehensive partnerships, for these necessarily span multiple units, departments, and schools, involving a variety of internal stakeholders in an external relationship with a partner. Senior international officers (SIOs) as well as partnership directors and managers will do well to assess their campus cultures prior to launching any institutional initiatives that intend to foster comprehensive partnership development. Those who find themselves in weak, internally oriented environments will need to use a variety of soft skills and acute cultural sensitivity to influence campus culture to become more internally cohesive and externally focused. Strategies for making these shifts include understanding the drivers and goals of various schools and units, identifying areas of horizontal alignment, and building on those connections of shared interest.

Institutions with weak central organizational support will likely face more initial challenges catalyzing and supporting effective comprehensive institutional partnerships for two key reasons. First, the institutional culture of decentralized governance and school- or unit-based independence will most often prevail, making it difficult to build strong connections across and between these various schools and units. In such contexts, partnership managers and directors may find themselves spending more time building internal connections and developing institutional cohesion rather than working with external partners, at least initially. While this may be frustrating, developing internal cohesion and fostering coordination is critical for comprehensive partnerships to grow, so it is time well spent.

Second, in decentralized contexts, the central international office is likely to be thinly staffed, which often encourages individual schools and units to develop or add resources to meet their own needs. In such cases, individual schools might add staffing resources to steward their priority international partners, further complicating the terrain for internal cohesion and external coherence. In these cases, SIOs and partnership managers should work with school deans and unit directors to understand their priorities, assess needs, manage expectations, and offer reasonable support. Senior leadership support is critical for making comprehensive international partnerships an institutional priority. From scattered, siloed, and rhizomatic structures, organizational strategies can be formed through internal collaboration and alignment. But the central international office needs staff members who can focus on partnership curation and development.

Trust and Familiarity in Partnership Development

Trust underpins an organization's ability to form alliances, share information, and develop common goals (Zheng 2015) with partners, and national as well as organizational cultures inform trust development. For a partnership to become active, and possibly generative, partners must have confidence that each will act as agreed (Zheng 2015). Trust builds through acts that develop and reaffirm this confidence. Thus, while general agreements to collaborate may originate from a place of mutual goodwill, without specificity and follow-through—which, together with goodwill, cultivate organizational trust—a true partnership will not flourish.

Key features of organizational trust include competence, reliability, and goodwill (Dyer 2000). Figure 2 outlines these key features, illustrating the elements that can be associated with each component.

Figure 2. Components and Artifacts of Organizational Trust

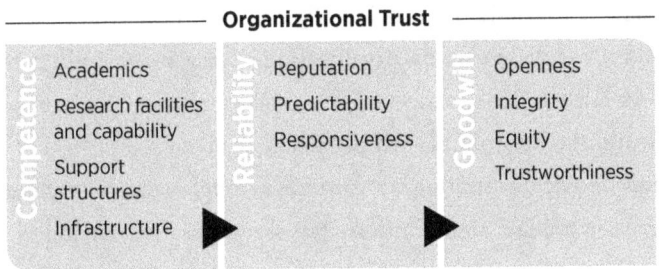

Source: Adapted from Dyer (2000).

Competence refers to the appropriateness of the partner—how successful will its participation make the various projects and initiatives to be undertaken through the collaboration? Competence is best initially assessed prior to engagement and can be accomplished via organizational research investigating the potential partner's academic and research capabilities, support structures, and infrastructure. Competence will be constantly recalibrated during the course of the collaboration, and, depending on the goals of the collaboration or the stage of development of one or more of the partners, competence in various areas may change over time.

To showcase institutional competence, partnership managers should ensure they have at their disposal an informational flyer or brochure on their institution, including key facts and figures such as the date founded, schools/academic units, academic and research strengths, rankings, recent awards and distinctions, and institutional demographics (i.e., student body and instructional faculty sizes and makeup). Also useful are admissions marketing materials and academic catalogs, which are especially valuable for student exchanges. Highlights of the strategic plan that are related to global engagement and priorities for engaging international partners (e.g., research priorities, academic program growth, etc.) and clear knowledge of how academic and research strengths align with the partner institution will also help to showcase the institution's competence as a partner.

Predictability, responsiveness, and reputation make up an institution's reliability quotient. These elements may be assessed prior to engagement most effectively by consultation with trusted internal and external sources or, to a lesser degree, via university rankings. Reliability will be continually reassessed during collaborative activities, particularly an institution's responsiveness and predictability. For these reasons, organizations that want to build partnerships for the long term must ensure they have the structures in place to manage communications and projects with partners effectively.

In addition to demonstrating competence through background research and informational materials, organizations can showcase their reliability by referring to tangible outcomes such as notable alumni, institutional distinctions, and awards received. Organizations will also be well served by knowing if any previous connections existed with a partner and, if so, the history of those connections. Prior to partner meetings, those leaders and staff members who are deputized to negotiate collaboration should apprise themselves of their own institutional protocols for formalizing relationships in agreements, including knowing whether and which templates exist and the signatory rules for agreements. Often these questions arise early in discussions for collaboration, and knowing one's own institutional practices demonstrates competence and reliability.

Reliability and competence both inform an organization's perceived goodwill—its openness, integrity, equity—and overall trustworthiness. If an organization is neither reliable nor competent, it will not be perceived by others as trustworthy, and its ability to be received with goodwill and, ultimately, to partner will be undermined. On the other hand, organizations that are seen as being both inherently reliable and competent—measured perhaps through notable alumni as well as top awards or rankings—will often find themselves showered with goodwill.

Institutions can help foster goodwill by referring to and drawing on alumni with ties to both institutions and, if appropriate culturally, bestowing small gifts upon institutional leaders and hosts during visits. More importantly, though, institutions should strive for equity in collaborative relationships by listening to the partner's needs and structuring programs and activities that create balanced collaborative structures. Building trust through iterative projects as part of a comprehensive relationship helps institutions move toward deep mutual understanding at the organizational level that will outlast any one individual or project involved.

Trust and Familiarity in Organizational Relationships

Collaborative relationships necessarily involve an element of risk. Thus, as institutions enter new markets and engage in research and academic collab-orations across borders, they must consider their risk toler-ance. Partnerships can temper this risk or elevate it, depending on how well the partners are suited and how the relation-ship is approached, structured, and managed. Some ventures necessarily involve more risk than others. Figure 3 depicts different types of relationships and connections, scaling them across the matrices of risk and trust and familiarity.

Figure 3. Trust-Risk Matrix

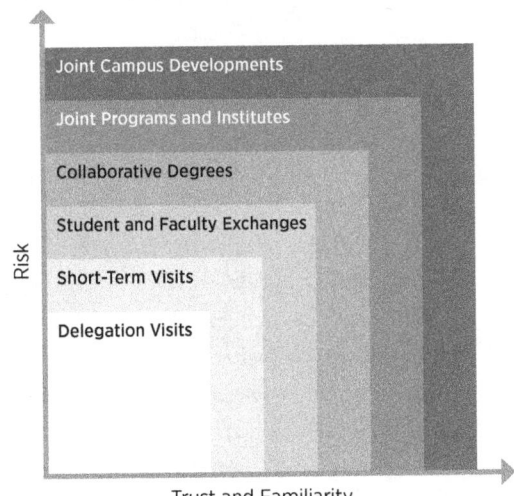

Risk

- Joint Campus Developments
- Joint Programs and Institutes
- Collaborative Degrees
- Student and Faculty Exchanges
- Short-Term Visits
- Delegation Visits

Trust and Familiarity

As the figure suggests, those connections that involve less familiarity also typically involve less risk. Equally, starting a relationship for a joint campus development from a position of unfamiliarity would be extremely risky, which is not to say this isn't done. Lack of familiarity significantly increases the risk involved in a collaboration because the partners have not gone through various cycles of funding and projects and exchanges together, learning how to work concurrently in the process. As suggested implicitly by the figure, building gradually to larger projects allows for a safer trajectory to develop mutual familiarity and trust.

Conclusion

Organizations that wish to develop long-term, comprehensive partnerships spanning disciplines and programs will want to organize themselves to cultivate relationships for longevity. This will involve institutional structures that support both short-term projects as well as those that may span years, in addition to developing administrative structures that foster individual projects and institutional connections. This diversity of engagement involves ensuring the presence of dynamic organizational structures and robust mechanisms to ingest and archive various forms of information related to institutional connections abroad.

References

American Council on Education. 2012. *Mapping Internationalization on U.S. Campuses: 2012 Edition.* Washington, DC: American Council on Education.

Dyer, Jeffrey. 2000. *Collaborative Advantage: Winning Through Extended Enterprise Supplier Networks.* Oxford, England: Oxford University Press.

Gatewood, Jane, and Susan Sutton. 2016. *International Partnerships: Part One: Definitions and Dimensions.* Internationalization in Action. Washington, DC: American Council on Education. https://www.acenet.edu/Documents/IIA-Intl-Partnerships-Part-1.pdf.

Helms, Robin Matross, and Lucia Brajkovic. 2017. *Mapping Internationalization on U.S. Campuses: 2017 Edition.* Washington, DC: American Council on Education. https://www.acenet.edu/Documents/Mapping-Internationalization-2017.pdf.

Knight, Jane. 2015. "Five Myths about Internationalization." *International Higher Education* 62. https://doi.org/10.6017/ihe.2011.62.8532.

Marinoni, Giorgio. 2019. *Internationalization of Higher Education: An Evolving Landscape, Locally and Globally.* International Association of Universities 5th Global Survey. Berlin: DUZ Academic Publishers.

Sandström, Anna-Malin, and Leasa Weimer. 2016. "International Strategic Partnerships." *EAIE Barometer.* European Association for International Education. https://www.eaie.org/our-resources/library/publication/Research-and-trends/international-strategic-partnerships.html.

Sporn, Barbara. 1996. "Managing University Culture: An Analysis of the Relationship Between Institutional Culture and Management Approaches." *Higher Education* 32, 41–61.

Zheng, Liu. 2015. "Trust Between Organizations: A Review of Current Research and Recommendation for the Future." *Review of Contemporary Business Research* 4, 1:40–48.

6

Corporate, Industry, and Nongovernmental Institutional Partnership Engagement

A CASE STUDY FROM UNIVERSITY OF SOUTH CAROLINA

Paul Allen Miller

n the United States, the relationship between higher education and the larger community in which it operates has fundamentally changed during the last 50 years. In the 1970s, most institutions of higher education were largely self-contained entities, with minimal interaction beyond the bounds of their campuses aside from well-defined, mission-oriented outreach such as the extension services run by land-grant universities. Most schools ran their own bookstores, cafeterias, and dormitories (Woodhouse 2015; Wood 2000). Community service was often limited to charities supported by fraternities and sororities. Distance education was in its infancy. Study abroad was largely a nascent idea, reserved for the privileged. International student recruitment was sporadic and haphazard at best. The ivory tower was not just an epithet used by critics of higher education; in some ways, it was the ideal.

There was a deliberate effort to insulate institutions of higher learning from the economic and political pressures of the larger world to preserve academic freedom and autonomy of thought. In that world, the very idea of a position such as the senior international officer (SIO) of a college or university was all but unthinkable. However, under the pressures of globalization, institutions have increasingly relied on outside entities to supplement their services and programs. These relationships often became formalized through partnership agreements. This chapter offers guidance on engaging in corporate, industry, and nongovernmental organization (NGO) partnerships by examining the need for them, the kinds of partnerships available, and best practices and concrete examples.

Historical Context

While higher education in the United States saw vast expansion in the 1950s and 1960s—with the number of students growing rapidly thanks to the GI Bill, the baby boom, and many state governments' commitment to low-cost higher education—in the 1970s, this trend began to shift. The emphasis was no longer on simply building more campuses, but, out of economic and strategic necessity, the focus was increasingly on how to run campuses more efficiently. It became obvious that there were certain things universities simply did not do well. Bookstores, food service, janitorial services, and housing were often cost centers, places where universities lost money and did not always provide good service.

In the 1980s and 1990s, it became common for institutions to ask outside businesses to assume different parts of their operations. Universities negotiated contracts whereby outside entities paid for the right to sell their goods and services on campus. Cost centers became income streams, even as universities lost some of the ability to control their own environment in the process. This period coincided with an increased emphasis under the Reagan administration on the necessity of running publicly supported higher education "like a business," along with decreased public support for taxes and spending on higher education. Among the results of these shifts was increased competition for students as tuition-paying "customers," who, in that new role, expected higher levels of service. There was also a growing need for colleges and universities to justify their practices to their larger communities and to engage those communities through service learning, economic development, and other forms of outreach, returning to the promises and assumptions of the Morrill Land-Grant acts (1862).

Lastly, this period saw the beginning and expansion of globalization with the end of the cold war, the opening of China, and the technology revolution, which vastly expanded communication and made possible global commerce on a scale previously unrealized. In this environment, to be a successful university increasingly meant having a global profile: recruiting international students, providing international opportunities for domestic students, partnering with international institutions, and promoting research and service opportunities around the world (see Di Leo 2013). The ivory tower surrounded by its ivy-clad walls had become a thing of the past, outside of a small number of well-endowed private institutions.

In this environment, a college or university SIO needs to be prepared to engage with a variety of off-campus entities, including service providers, corporate and university partners, and NGOs.

The Need for Partnerships

There was a time when, if a U.S. public university needed to make a major investment, it would make the proposal for a capital expenditure—whether it was a building, a piece of administrative infrastructure, or a new student-centered initiative—to the governmental body that oversaw it. The university would have a reasonable expectation of receiving that funding, if the expenditure had a strong justification and was not deemed extravagant. Today's universities, however, are expected to be largely self-sufficient.

The Higher Education Landscape

While the percentage of funding that individual universities receive varies from state to state, the overall declines of public funding are well documented (American Academy of Arts & Sciences 2015; Mitchell, Leachman, and Masterson 2017). For example, at the University of South Carolina (UofSC), 20 years ago, 50 percent of the budget came from state allocation; today, it is less than 10 percent. Although similar trends can be seen throughout those parts of the Western world where the neoliberal model of funding higher education has been ascendant, other nations, particularly in Asia, have been investing heavily in their university and research infrastructure during this same period. Between 2007 and 2017, China added more than 700 new institutions of higher education and has set a goal of becoming a net exporter of higher education (Han 2019; Wenyu 2017; Bevins and Philips 2017; Kuo 2013).

These developments have meant that when U.S. universities have needed to make major capital outlays for large items or systems, they have had to turn to a growing number of private partners that have the funding to make these outlays possible. This shift in financial resources is evident in the rising number of public-private partnerships developed for the purposes of building residence halls, providing study abroad support, and recruiting international students.

Effects of Internationalization

Colleges and universities now must have a global presence in order to compete for students, researchers, and resources. However, the outlays required to transform a regional institution into an international one can be both hard to come by and difficult to justify to stakeholders concerned about rising tuition and serving the local population. Yet, internationalization requires capital.

Successful international student recruitment cannot be accomplished simply by having a nice website or attending the occasional fair. It requires having staff on the ground in targeted markets, touting the university's global reputation and offerings. By the same token, international research collaboration requires travel and the cultivation of a network of alumni, administrative, and faculty connections. International recruitment and research collaboration are often implicitly or explicitly predicated on international rankings, which are, in turn, often based on international reputation, international student enrollment, and the internationalization of the faculty. It can be difficult to establish an international presence on one's own steam and without considerable expense, so partnerships are crucial.

Strategic Partnership Development

Partners, by definition, have their own agendas. One way that universities can avoid being pushed into serving agendas that are not their own is by being very clear about their own goals, long-term strategies, and short-term tactics, which usually appear in some form of a published strategic plan. There may also be a variety of periodic announcements of short-term priorities and long-term visions that can come in the form of presidential addresses, announcements by the provost, or various high-level white papers. Such statements can provide a road map for the internationalization of the campus.

From there, it is possible to formulate a more individualized strategic plan for the internationalization of the university. The goals set will determine the kinds of partnership that make sense for a given institution and can provide a compass for navigating the necessary compromises entailed within a partner relationship.

Stakeholder Support

A plan only has force if it has the support of the larger community. This begins with the process of formulating it. It is imperative to have a representative body draft the plan, with both faculty and staff input. The faculty members elected to participate must represent the major interests on campus that would benefit from or have jurisdiction over various internationalization efforts. Once the plan has been drafted, the SIO must seek the support of the upper administration. This is one reason why it is crucial to begin by aligning the plan with stated university objectives. But while such alignment is vital, it is equally important to have the active personal support of the president and provost, or analogous positions within a given university system. If the upper leadership of the institution are not bought into the strategic vision of the plan, it can be very difficult to overcome the institutional and bureaucratic inertia that is able to undo even the most well-crafted proposal.

Once this agreement has been secured, it is essential in a large institution to gain the support of the deans. At large, healthy institutions, deans are seldom micromanaged and have the ability to either advance or derail the best-laid plans. Thus, SIOs must be able to demonstrate how their strategic plan aligns with the more specific interests of each college and school.

Lastly, even though faculty were involved in the initial drafting of the strategic plan, that will normally include a representative few. It is important to build faculty members' support on the larger scale because they will be the ones to actually execute the initiatives. Faculty buy-in can be gained through traditional faculty governance, collegiate and provostial retreats, workshops, and other forms of outreach.

Faculty support is crucial because there is often a great deal of misapprehension and resistance to university partnerships. Faculty members are understandably resistant to ceding academic control to any outside entity, and especially to those motivated by primarily commercial interests. Therefore, it is imperative to listen to those concerns and be able to demonstrate at each step of the way that any such partnership is undertaken only because it aligns with the strategic goals of the institution.

With support from across the various groups of stakeholders, the SIO and the international office are then in a position to communicate and defend those goals and interests to their potential partners. It is also important to recognize that partners have their own legitimate interests, and there is no reason not to expect them to pursue those interests. Whether an institution is working with a small study abroad provider, a network of international recruiters, or a large corporation like IBM, Siemens, or Volvo, every organization has its own institutional dynamic and goals.

The failure to recognize this fact can lead to either undue suspicion of the motives of the partner (i.e., the partner must be up to something because it is not always acting in what the institution has defined as its best interests) or naiveté about the goals of the partner (i.e., the partner will naturally want to do what is in the best interests of the institution). Both extremes can be best guarded against by having clarity about the institution's goals, ensuring there is strong support for those goals, and communicating them clearly to the institution's partners, while listening to, supporting, and, where possible, fostering the goals of the partner. Every partnership involves both opportunity and compromise.

University Partnerships

Partnerships come in many shapes and sizes, and each configuration has its own set of dynamics and needs that must be managed. University partnerships can range from the exchange of researchers, faculty, and students to dual- and joint-degree programs to large multilateral partnerships that involve multiple universities, corporate partners, and governmental agencies. These affiliations often begin from the humble memorandum of understanding (MOU). But the more complex and comprehensive partnerships are seldom born fully fledged and often take years of patient cultivation, relationship building, and the establishment of mutual trust.

It is important that there is clear communication between all partners from the beginning. Foreign universities often operate under very different regulatory regimes than do U.S. universities, and their financial assumptions may be very different as well. In some parts of the world, particularly in Africa, Latin America, and the Middle East, for example, private for-profit universities are much more common than they are in the United States and are a central part of the higher education landscape. A university that might shy away from partnering with a for-profit institution in the United States, fearing the reputational consequences, may be open to it in another national context in which such universities are part of the norm.

Government, Corporate, Industry, and Nongovernmental Organization Partnerships

Aside from the traditional approach of partnering with other institutions of higher education, many colleges and universities have developed productive, sustainable relationships with government, corporate, industry, and NGO partners, who offer different forms of expertise and services.

Government Partners

One effective way to build a constituency for internationalizing the university is to partner with a state or local governmental agency that is charged with economic development. The presence of a university partner can be an asset for Departments of Commerce seeking foreign direct investment in a specific region, looking to develop a research economy, or hoping to open new markets overseas. These agencies have their own agendas and are often not looking to support higher education per se, but they can provide entrées to institutions while building political support at home. They can also provide funding for specific initiatives or for general research, as found in initiatives like North Carolina's Research Triangle.

Many universities work closely with these agencies to expand their opportunities. The University of Georgia, for example, has close relationships with a variety of international partners (including Brazil, Korea, and the United Kingdom) that have been facilitated through the Georgia Department of Economic Development. Similarly, the German government sponsors a variety of national research initiatives aimed specifically at economic development, including the network of Fraunhofer Institutes discussed below.

Collaborations with foreign governmental agencies can produce considerable benefits to both parties and open up other avenues for collaboration.

At UofSC, for example, the College of Social Work has developed a close working relationship with the Ministry of Labor, Invalids, and Social Affairs in Vietnam. They work together on capacity building to develop social work as a profession, which previously did not exist in the country. Vietnam was chosen due to faculty ties and the needs of the country.

Whether at home or abroad, relationships with governmental agencies are frequently dependent on the political environment and personalities involved. Those factors are subject to change, and institutions of higher education need to make sure that they manage risk accordingly. It is important to have detailed knowledge of the situation and ensure broad institutional buy-in so that large initiatives are not dependent on the presence of one or two personalities. Agreements should be subject to periodic review by both sides so that changing circumstances can be acknowledged and mutually agreeable changes implemented.

Corporate and Industry Partners

Similarly, corporate and industry partnerships can bring real value to institutions. These relationships come in two primary forms. On the one hand, private partnerships may provide a service that the university has decided it cannot do efficiently and effectively, such as providing logistical and risk management assistance for students studying abroad, fielding and managing a network of international recruiters, or building residence halls and managing food service. On the other hand, there can be more nuanced symbiotic relationships with businesses and corporations whereby universities become sites for privately funded research, for fostering start-ups, and for workforce training.

As partnerships grow and deepen, what sometimes began as a mere service provider relationship can develop into something more complex. It is important to remember, however, that private corporations have a fiduciary duty to their shareholders and, while such partnerships can be very useful for both parties, it is rare that their interests coincide completely.

Nongovernmental Organization Partners

NGOs can be very effective partners for colleges and universities. Many international service-learning projects work with a variety of local and international actors, ranging from organizations such as Doctors Without Borders, Engineers Without Borders, and Hope for Children to local religious organizations and charities. Often, these groups may form partnerships with corporations, service providers, and governmental agencies as well.

Universities wishing to have an impact and to nurture their international profile would do well to include NGOs within their partnership portfolios. They should choose reputable NGOs with established track records and organizations whose values align with those of the home institution.

Case Study Examples: University of South Carolina

At this point, it will be useful to move from theory to practice and talk about some specific case studies, drawn from the experience of the University of South Carolina. While no institution's experience is typical, many face common challenges, including increasing student recruitment and education abroad opportunities. UofSC made the strategic decision to find partners in government, corporations and industry, and NGOs to enhance its student population, curricular offerings, and internationalization portfolio.

International Student Recruitment

After a period of reflection and after seeking to move the needle on its own, UofSC found it useful to partner with Shorelight Education to increase significantly its international student body. For many years, UofSC's undergraduate international enrollment had been essentially flat, with many of those students on scholarship or receiving some other form of reduced tuition. UofSC needed a means to expand its international enrollment, but one that would not require the capital outlay required to stand up a network of agents and recruiters on its own. It was also preferable that these students pay as close to full nonresident tuition as possible.

While there are many possible partners in this field, and many with good reputations and results, the university has found this partnership with Shorelight Education to be particularly fruitful because UofSC has been able to retain academic control over all aspects of the program. The English as a second language courses are staffed by UofSC's English Programs for Internationals, which has been in existence for 40 years and is accredited by the Commission on English Language Accreditation. The students in the International Accelerator Program are taught exclusively by UofSC faculty using UofSC syllabi and materials. The academic director of the International Accelerator Program is a UofSC employee. The students are part of a UofSC program that is managed and supported by the university. They are not segregated from UofSC students or staff.

The ability to maintain strict academic control of the program has made it easier to retain support at the faculty and dean levels. The program has been able to maintain a freshman to sophomore retention rate and a class GPA that is at, or above that of, the general student population. At the same time, the program has been able to double UofSC's international undergraduate enrollment and grow its master's-level enrollment in a financially sustainable fashion.

Study Abroad Opportunities

Another area in which public-private partnerships are common is the use of providers for study abroad programs. Providers can be an invaluable source of logistical and academic support for universities looking to increase and deepen their students' abroad experiences. Some providers also offer significant assistance in the area of risk management abroad. In some cases, however, the use of provider organizations can increase costs for students, and the providers' academic contacts and resources may not be at the level of what would be expected by the home institution.

UofSC uses a mixture of different kinds of partners to augment its overseas programming. UofSC established its Global UofSC program to offer a series of sites around the world devoted to specific clusters of disciplines where the university plans to return to each year. One of the most successful has been UofSC in Costa Rica: Global Health, a collaborative program built between faculty in the departments of public health, medicine, and Spanish. Working together with one of the leading providers, International Studies Abroad (ISA), an initial three-week program (with an optional fourth week) was established in which students do coursework taught by UofSC faculty and perform community service and research in a local nursing home, an AIDS treatment facility, or one of Costa Rica's largest public hospitals.

In this model of collaboration, the private partner arranges the homestays and logistics, while allowing the university to have a very light footprint. At the same time, significant relationships have grown between local governmental and nongovernmental organizations and university faculty. The program is now at capacity and, in accordance with UofSC's long-term plan, options are being explored to expand the program and create a more permanent presence for UofSC in Costa Rica.

While for Costa Rica, a private partner was the right answer, at another site in the same series, UofSC in the Galapagos: Sustainability, the decision was made to work with a university partner. To this day, the Universidad de San Francisco de Quito (USFQ) has the only campus allowed in the Galapagos. Beyond its extraordinary beauty and unique wildlife, the fragile environment of the Galapagos poses very directly the problem of how to marry economic development and tourism, with sustainable management practices.

Working together with USFQ, faculty in the departments of hospitality and tourism, geography, marine science, and environmental science have created a unique learning environment for a limited number of students. As in Costa Rica, it began as a three-week program and quickly reached capacity. UofSC now has a direct enrollment semester program with USFQ and is pursuing a variety of joint research projects with faculty members from the two institutions. The program was made possible due to a faculty member's connections with both USFQ and the government of Ecuador; the faculty member's academic specialty was in sustainable tourism.

As these two cases make clear, there is no one answer that is right in all cases concerning partnerships in study abroad, but SIOs and other university administrators must make judgments on a case-by-case basis, grounded in a clearly articulated strategic vision possessing the support of both the participating faculty and the administration.

Business Incubators

Partnerships between universities and private companies and corporations—who are not in a direct service provider relationship such as those in the case of student recruitment and study abroad—can come in many forms and degrees of complexity. The simplest are one-on-one partnerships on campus. Many universities around the world, for example, have business incubators. Georgia Tech's Research Institute (GRTI) and the research park outside the University of Liverpool all work to incubate and spin off companies. Similar facilities can be found at the various campuses of Tec de Monterrey, to say nothing of those linked to Berkeley and Stanford in northern California's Silicon Valley. National Chung Hsing University in Taichung, Taiwan, is located adjacent to the Central Taiwan Research Park, often called Taiwan's Silicon Valley.

These are sites where students and faculty members can take ideas developed in the laboratory or the classroom and turn them into entrepreneurial start-ups. By partnering with local economic development agencies, chambers of commerce, and established businesses, these business incubators provide a safe space to discuss ideas, work on common problems, and receive the coaching and advice that help guide nascent businesses from mere ideas to freestanding entities.

While many examples could be given, from the perspective of internationalization, one of the most interesting at UofSC is Varna International, a world-recognized concert tour organizer specializing in custom-tailored performance tours and music training academies throughout Europe, the Mediterranean, and the United States. Varna International began in UofSC's business incubator and now books concerts around the world, raising the profile of the university. Business incubators show that the partnerships between universities and industry are not one-way propositions in which universities merely purchase from or provide services for external entities. Rather, institutions of higher education can also create and nurture small businesses that have a global impact.

Research Opportunities

Many colleges and universities also partner with large, well-established corporations. IBM, for example, occupies two floors of one of UofSC's major research buildings. The Center for Applied Innovation and Advanced Analytics, Watson Internet of Things, and Watson Health Businesses are housed at UofSC, and each provides faculty and students with new opportunities to develop their talents and skills with real-world applications, while also contracting to provide information technology services for the university. The Center for Applied Innovation leverages information derived from the internet of things to study a wide range of phenomena and develop predictive analytics around them. Projects range from conditions-based maintenance for aircraft—where tiny sensors can predict equipment failure before it happens and help direct maintenance teams—to sensors in the neonatal intensive care unit that alert doctors to a premature infant's changing health status.

UofSC researchers are working with their IBM counterparts and engaging with international and transnational corporations like Boeing, Michelin, and Volvo. This is a fundamentally different relationship from that of a service provider, although that can still be one aspect of the relationship. In this case, the university is engaged in business development at the same time as the corporate partner is promoting and funding research that has both academic value and direct application in a complex global economy. The university not only gains funding and produces research, but its global and international profile is also enhanced in ways that directly support its goals. Most of the research conducted falls under the Fundamental Research Exclusion and enjoys the same rights of academic freedom and publication as publicly funded research, although more narrow proprietary research is not excluded.

Another example of this kind of international corporate partnership can be seen in Siemens's recent gift to UofSC. Siemens is a German conglomerate headquartered in Berlin and Munich. It is the largest industrial manufacturing company in Europe, with branch offices around the world. In June 2017, UofSC received an in-kind gift of $628 million in Product Lifecycle Management software from Siemens. Siemens has also given hardware to UofSC, creating the UofSC Siemens Digital Factory Innovation Lab, a first of its kind in the country, where future engineers can be trained on Siemens systems during their education at UofSC. Faculty are also receiving training on how to integrate the software and hardware into the curriculum.

Siemens's donation means that students in UofSC's College of Engineering and Computing have access to industry-standard software and hardware throughout the course of their studies, unleashing their talents to create world-class engineers and designers. What Siemens receives in return is a fully constructed demonstration laboratory, where, instead of showing potential clients a PowerPoint presentation or a video, they can bring them to campus and display the systems in action. The university, thus, becomes an international showroom for Siemens's technology and research prowess. This partnership also provides the opportunity for future research collaborations between engineers at Siemens, UofSC, and other partners, including IBM.

Multilateral Partnerships

While this initial group of partnerships concentrated on relationships occurring on campus and emphasized one-to-one relationships between businesses and the university, other, more complex configurations are possible. In fact, in a globalized economy, international university partners often offer their domestic counterparts access to corporate partners both at home and abroad.

Jönköping University and Volvo

UofSC has had a relationship with Jönköping University in Sweden since 2011. This began as an exchange relationship with UofSC's International Business Program. After a series of high-level visits by both sides, the decision was made to move beyond business to include engineering and to move beyond traditional student exchange to include reciprocal internships and collaboration with international businesses. The timing of this new collaboration was made propitious by the opening of a Volvo plant just outside the port of Charleston in South Carolina.

Foreign direct investment had long been an important part of the economic development strategy of the South Carolina Department of Commerce. Thus, the university's ability to work with these new industries not only allowed for a corporate partnership but also directly served the policy interests of the state, making the university a valued partner at a time when state support for higher education has been less than robust.

Jönköping already had an existing relationship with Volvo, whose head-quarters is located in the nearby city of Gothenburg. At the same time, Husqvarna—the Swedish lawn, home, and construction equipment manu-facturer—already had a major facility in Orangeburg, South Carolina, half-way between Columbia, where the university is located, and Charleston. Husqvarna was founded in the city of the same name, immediately adjacent to Jönköping (they are now incorporated into a single municipality). As dis-cussions with Jönköping developed, it became clear that there were possibil-ities for reciprocal internships, with UofSC students having the ability to go to Sweden and work in the facilities of Husqvarna and Volvo, and Jönköping students able to do the same in South Carolina.

The projects these students would work on would be applied research for the companies in question, and this work would need to be supervised by their professors, which would in turn open up the possibility for direct research collaborations between the universities and their corporate partners on both continents. Thus, what had begun as a simple exchange relationship had the potential to grow into a more substantial program of student and faculty mobility, joint research, and state-supported economic development, allowing the university to advance in its three primary missions of teaching, research, and service, while furthering its strategic goals in internationalization.

Sister-State Agreements

As another form of multilateral partnership, many states and localities have sister-state and sister-city agreements around the world. Massachusetts, for example, maintains a sister-state relationship with Baden-Württemberg in Germany. California claims to have no less than 48 such agreements, while New Jersey has nine. Sometimes these are little more than goodwill gestures, excuses for signing ceremonies and trips, or pieces of paper that are filed away in a drawer. But, like university MOUs, they can also be the first step in a more sustained collaborative relationship. These agreements create webs of potential relationships that can then be leveraged for a wide range of purposes.

For example, the state of South Carolina became sister states with Rhineland Palatinate in Germany in 1997. Each locality faced a common problem. The

United States was realigning its military forces in the aftermath of the cold war and was closing military bases both at home and abroad. Many U.S. bases located in the part of southern Germany that makes up Rhineland Palatinate were closed, and the South Carolina economy was particularly hard hit by the closing of the Charleston naval yard.

The initial sister-state agreement centered on repurposing these closed military facilities for civilian economic purposes. The agency that led this effort on the South Carolina side was the State Budget and Control Board, which reported to the legislature. The Commerce Department had already successfully brought a major BMW manufacturing plant to South Carolina from the state of Bavaria. Moreover, within Rhineland Palatinate, the city of Kaiserslautern had also become a sister city with Columbia, South Carolina. There are two universities within Kaiserslautern, one of which, the Technical University of Kaiserslautern, possessed a Fraunhofer Institute. The Fraunhofer Institutes are a network of applied research facilities sponsored by the German government that specialize in doing work tied directly to industrial purposes and often receive funding from industry. The Fraunhofer Institutes now have branches in other countries, including the United States.

Fred Monk, a former journalist who had worked for a number of years with the South Carolina Department of Commerce and in various forms of economic development, conceived of the idea in the early 2000s that the sister-state agreement could be leveraged to create a Fraunhofer Institute in South Carolina that would unite the state's two major research universities, Clemson University and UofSC, with the Fraunhofer Institute in Kaiserslautern to power research-driven economic development for the state. There were a number of attempts over the years, but, as is common in such complex undertakings, there were personnel changes, shifts in priorities, a major economic disruption in 2008, and other assorted vicissitudes that made the project hard to bring to fruition. Nonetheless, Monk persisted and, in 2016, UofSC sent a delegation with Monk to Kaiserslautern and an initial MOU was signed.

For the past 2 years, the South Carolina Department of Commerce and UofSC have been using this relationship to leverage South Carolina's sister-state relationship in Rhineland Palatinate to spur innovation and technological development. The goal is to help companies grow in the digital economy by using the talent at the universities. The initial work is focused in the areas of rapid innovation, cybersecurity, and telemedicine. The South Carolina Department of Commerce is working with the Fraunhofer Institute for Experimental Software Engineering in Kaiserslautern, the Fraunhofer Center for Experimental Software Engineering at the University of Maryland, UofSC, and Clemson University to create the South Carolina Center for Innovation in a bid to foster the next generation of industry and business for the state.

Initial projects of the South Carolina Center for Innovation have included work for Bicycle Corporation of America, BMW, Palmetto Health Systems, Safran Industries, and the South Carolina Center for Logistics. Dedicated seed funding has been provided by the South Carolina Department of Commerce. Each of these projects combine corporate talent, university faculty, graduate students, and others to develop solutions, new systems, and new products whose precise status and ownership will be negotiated in individual agreements. But having now established this framework, UofSC and the South Carolina Department of Commerce are looking for new collaborators around the world, particularly in the area of cybersecurity.

Partnerships Overseas

While the previous examples have looked primarily at partnerships that at least notionally centered around the main campus of the university, this final section examines a partnership located overseas. Of course, many universities have opened international campuses, and some of these have been successful. But many have also faced challenges ranging from changing local regulatory and political environments to insufficient enrollment. It can be very difficult to make a success of these ventures without a local sponsor, be that governmental or private.

One venture that has proven successful for UofSC has been an executive international master of business administration dual degree offered by UofSC and Chonnam National University in South Korea. This program is offered exclusively for executives chosen by the Korean Electric Power Corporation (KEPCO), which pays all tuition and fees. The program facilitates the development of international managers' critical skills and provides a unique chance for the students to study from a truly international perspective. UofSC has one of the strongest international business programs in the United States, but it offers relatively little coursework specific to the energy sector. Chonnam, however, has a strength in this field. This collaboration allows the two universities to play to their strong points while ensuring a steady funding stream.

KEPCO benefits from being able to develop its executive talent and prepare its employees to work in an increasingly interconnected global business environment. All the instruction takes place in Korea, with UofSC faculty visiting to offer courses and providing supplementary instruction via telepresence. This has proven to be a financially stable model that has allowed the university to raise its international profile with very low risk, while also increasing international enrollment and developing a growing alumni base on the Korean peninsula.

Conclusion

Partnerships are a permanent feature of today's higher education landscape. In the current funding environment for public higher education, partnerships are both a fiscal necessity and an opportunity for colleges and universities to broaden the range of their student experiences, diversify their student body, manage risk, fund research, and promote the economic development of the communities they serve.

However, it is critical to keep in mind that university and corporate cultures can be very different. Universities cannot afford to be profligate in their resources, their primary imperative is never profit, and their fiduciary duty is to their students, their faculty, and the communities that support them rather than their shareholders. At the same time, while state support has substantially diminished for public universities, the same cannot be said of state regulations, so major research universities often operate under a regulatory burden that makes rapid decisionmaking difficult if not impossible when compared to private industry. Moreover, in such complex multilateral partnerships, the cultural differences are not simply between public and private but also between diverse national business, university, and governmental cultures.

SIOs and university administrators focused on the bottom line need to recognize that these relationships are long-term investments that, when successful, will pay off over years, not months. Not all of these partnerships will succeed, but when they do, they can significantly serve the university's primary mission and advance its strategic interests, opening up possibilities of collaboration that were not envisioned under more traditional rubrics.

References

American Academy of Arts & Sciences. 2015. *Public Research Universities: Changes in State Funding.* Cambridge, MA: American Academy of Arts & Sciences. https://www.amacad.org/sites/default/files/publication/downloads/PublicResearchUniv_ChangesInStateFunding.pdf.

Bevins, Vincent, and Tom Phillips. 2017. "'Going Global': China Exports Soft Power with First Large-Scale University in Malaysia." *Guardian.* July 6, 2017. https://www.theguardian.com/world/2017/jul/07/going-global-china-exports-soft-power-with-first-large-scale-university-in-malaysia.

Di Leo, Jeffrey R. 2013. *Corporate Humanities in Higher Education: Moving Beyond the Neoliberal Academy.* New York, NY: Palgrave Macmillan.

Han, Shu. 2019. "Education in China – Statistics & Facts." Statista. November 22, 2019. https://www.statista.com/topics/2090/education-in-china.

Kuo, Lily. 2013. "The Next Phase of China's Global Soft Power Push Is Exporting Higher Education." Quartz. June 19, 2013. https://qz.com/96011/the-next-phase-of-chinas-global-soft-power-push-is-exporting-higher-education.

Mitchell, Michael, Michael Leachman, and Kathleen Masterson. 2017. "A Lost Decade in Higher Education Funding State Cuts Have Driven Up Tuition and Reduced Quality." Washington, DC: Center on Budget and Policy Priorities. https://www.cbpp.org/sites/default/files/atoms/files/2017_higher_ed_8-22-17_final.pdf.

Wenyu, Sun. 2017. "China's Higher Education Enrollment Rate Reaches 42.7 Per Cent in 2016." *People's Daily Online.* July 11, 2017. http://en.people.cn/n3/2017/0711/c90000-9240278.html.

Wood, Patricia A. 2000. "Outsourcing in Higher Education." ERIC Digest. Washington, DC: ERIC Clearinghouse on Higher Education. George Washington University Graduate School of Education and Human Development.

Woodhouse, Kellie. 2015. "How to Outsource." *Insider Higher Ed.* July 21, 2015. https://www.insidehighered.com/news/2015/07/21/institutions-outsource-they-should-keep-their-mission-and-vendor-close.

An Approach to International Agreements
A CASE STUDY FROM UNIVERSITY OF CALIFORNIA, DAVIS

Joanna Regulska, Jolynn Shoemaker, and Elizabeth Langridge-Noti

Many universities have experienced a proliferation in the number of agreements signed during recent years. The number of international agreements is often highlighted by universities as a simple metric to illustrate internationalization. The emphasis, in some cases, has been on quantity and lengthy lists of partners, rather than on quality and the depth of these relationships, which are more difficult to assess. Larger numbers of agreements do not necessarily indicate that partnerships are active or productive. A proliferation of agreements can also lead to institutional problems if adequate processes for the creation and tracking of agreements are not in place.

International agreements, however, are one important tool for facilitating, managing, and tracking joint activities between universities and their partners in other countries. Formalized agreements are valuable for a university in a number of ways:

- Agreements can mitigate legal liabilities and prevent misunderstandings by clearly articulating the intent of the university and its partners;

- Agreements can provide concrete documentation to show the existence of partnerships between institutions, whereas informal relationships are important but "invisible" on an institutional level;

- Agreements can support university branding, illustrating the university's commitment to internationalization and engagement with particular countries, regions, and issues; and

- Agreements can catalyze new collaborations or lead to the deepening of collaborations.

The majority of university international agreements have traditionally been bilateral (between two institutions). However, complex global challenges, often referred to as "wicked" problems due to their complexity, require multiple partners and the involvement of different stakeholders, including nongovernmental organizations (NGOs), government entities, and industry partners. This shifting partnership space has required new thinking about partnerships and how agreements can best facilitate university goals.

This chapter illustrates the international agreements management process employed at the University of California, Davis, which was designed to establish a uniform and streamlined operating procedure, a centralized platform of data, and an assessment structure to track the impact of collaborations.

A New International Agreements Process

The University of California, Davis (UC Davis) is one of 10 campuses in the public University of California (UC) system. The mission of the University of California as a public research university includes the creation, dissemination, preservation, and application of knowledge for the betterment of the global society.

UC Davis is committed to internationalization and has been making robust efforts to increase collaborations and partnerships in every region of the world. International agreements remain a critical mechanism in the university's internationalization efforts. The UC Office of the President establishes overall policy relating to international activities and determines which activities must be approved at various levels of the UC system and campus leadership. However, the UC system allows for campus and location autonomy to develop international partnerships consistent with the focus and needs of the campus or location.

In 2014–15, UC Davis began to discuss the development of new guidelines for international agreements. It was clear that the expansion and deepening of international university partnerships, and growing involvement of individuals and units across campus as part of internalization, required a more systematic approach for the future. Clarifying processes and facilitating internal coordination would support compliance and risk mitigation, while also creating new opportunities for collaborations and funding support globally. There was consensus among leadership that this was an opportune time to clarify and streamline the process for the campus community. The following needs were identified:

- Order: UC Davis needed a common framework or operating procedure for agreements, as there were many different forms of agreements and individual approaches among faculty and departments.

- Authority: UC Davis needed to promote a shared understanding of delegated authorities, so that campus leadership was aware of the development of agreements and that agreements were vetted before they were signed on behalf of the university.

- Tracking: UC Davis needed a centralized platform to gather accurate data on formalized international partnerships across the university in order to identify potential areas of strength in collaboration.

- Assessment: UC Davis needed a structure that could support the evaluation of the impact of international collaborations that were supported by the agreements.

UC Davis approached this process with several important parameters in mind. First, UC Davis is a land-grant university and this history and designation informs the university mission, structure, and priorities. UC Davis's international partnership goals, decisions, processes, and operating procedures would need to reflect the responsibilities of this designation. Additionally, the process would need to support the strategic priorities of UC Davis. UC Davis also needed to develop a process that worked for the university's shared governance structure and organizational norms in order to be sustainable and successful in the long term. Faculty needed to be a central part of the planning, from the beginning, to ensure that the process would be accepted and utilized widely. Finally, the process would have to be nimble enough to respond to the rapid changes that were taking place in universities and in the international context, which were affecting the very nature of both individual collaborations and university partnerships.

Stakeholder Engagement on Campus

In winter 2015, UC Davis created the Agreement Process Working Group (APWG). This launched a process that took more than 2 years to complete. From the beginning, the process was designed to include relevant stakeholders across campus, and it required multiple stages of discussion, drafting, and approvals. It also needed to take into account University of California systemwide policies. As a part of the UC system, UC Davis and all of its international activities, including agreements with foreign entities, must follow UC policies as well as relevant campus policies (www.ucgo.org/relevant-uc-policies-and-guidance).

The APWG charge was as follows:

> To develop procedures and processes for handling the various international contracts and agreements that require approval, concurrence or input from the Chancellor and Provost.

> To develop uniform procedures and processes, including identifying legal authorities for execution of such agreements, to:

> (1) ensure efficient negotiation and approval of such documents from the initial stages through signature at whatever level is necessary, including obtaining timely input from all interested parties;

> (2) monitor the progress, utility, and value of the agreement, including identifying an avenue for addressing any issues that may arise during its term; and

> (3) effectively and efficiently coordinating any appropriate modification or termination of the agreement, including handling any residual issues.

In spring 2015, a subgroup was created to draft the guidelines for international agreements and the agreement templates. The group was inclusive of various academic units and administrative offices that were heavily involved in partnership development and implementation internationally. The involvement of relevant campus stakeholders was a critical component of the APWG and the success of the process.

Campus Representation in the Agreement Process Working Group

The UC Davis international agreement process included a number of administrative and academic offices across campus. Units were chosen to participate in the process based on their involvement in international engagement. The College of Agricultural and Environmental Sciences, the School of Veterinary Medicine, and UC Davis Health were represented because they already managed multiple international agreements and had established offices to manage and support international engagement. Other offices managed other types of agreements, such as the Office of Research and Contracting Services.

AGREEMENT PROCESS WORKING GROUP (APWG) MEMBERS

- Academic Senate
- Campus Counsel
- Office of Chancellor and Provost
- College of Agricultural and Environmental Sciences
- Continuing and Professional Education
- Office of Corporate Relations
- Development and Alumni Relations
- Global Affairs
- Graduate Studies
- Office of Policy and Compliance
- Office of Procurement and Contracting Services
- Real Estate Services

- Office of Research
  - Research Compliance and Integrity
  - Sponsored Programs Office
- Risk Management
- School of Medicine/UC Davis Health
- School of Veterinary Medicine

APWG SUBWORK GROUP MEMBERS

- Campus Counsel
- Office of Chancellor and Provost/ Academic Senate Representative
- College of Agricultural and Environmental Sciences
- Continuing and Professional Education
- Office of Corporate Relations
- Global Affairs
- Office of Research
- School of Veterinary Medicine

Development of the Agreements Process

In winter 2016, the APWG produced a first draft of an agreements process that would centralize the facilitation, collection, and assessment of international agreements undertaken at UC Davis. The draft also needed to take into account a newly revised (summer 2017) systemwide University of California International Activities Policy (policy.ucop.edu/doc/2300651/ InternationalActivities). The purpose of the new systemwide policy was to "support the academic mission by encouraging and supporting international collaboration, education, exploration, research, and service; provide an administrative framework for international activities so that they can be established expeditiously and operate effectively; direct proponents of international activities to consider and address the risks of international engagement; protect the reputation of the University; and guard the interests of faculty, other academic appointees, students, and staff while engaging in international activities."

This APWG draft was shared with campuswide stakeholders through summer 2017 and submitted to the UC Davis Academic Senate in fall 2017, pursuant to the UC Davis Senate Consultation Policy, for comment, response, and approval. The new campus process was approved by the UC Davis Academic Senate in spring 2018. The new policy and process launched in summer 2018.

The APWG created a streamlined process for the facilitation of new and renewed international agreements that run through a central, identified office, Global Affairs. This new process resulted in the need for additional administrative support to manage all of the related tasks. Initially, an agreements/partnership manager was shared with the Office of Research, given the resource limitations and overlapping needs of the two units in facilitating international collaboration. More recently, as the acceptance of the new process spreads throughout the campus, Global Affairs has recognized the need for a dedicated agreements manager to manage the workload generated from a campus with 10 schools and colleges. Close collaboration is maintained with the Office of Research through a dedicated international agreements manager in each office. New relationships are being built with recognized point people for agreements in schools and colleges as well.

Implementation of the International Agreements Process

The UC Davis international agreements process requires a faculty champion for every new agreement and provides guidelines and templates for basic, nonbinding agreements that have been preapproved by the Office of the Campus Counsel. Figure 1 illustrates the steps involved in the process.

Figure 1. The UC Davis International Agreement Proposal and Approval Process

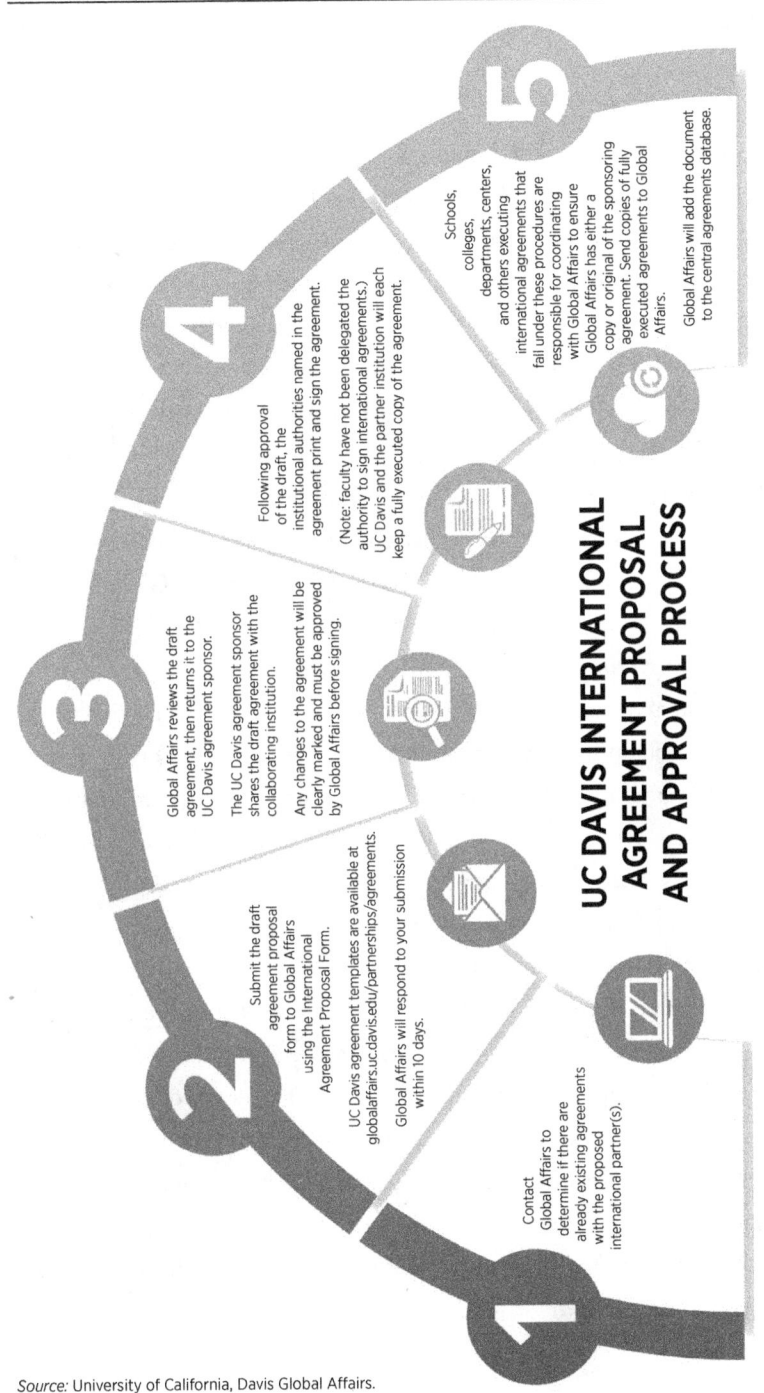

UC DAVIS INTERNATIONAL AGREEMENT PROPOSAL AND APPROVAL PROCESS

1 Contact Global Affairs to determine if there are already existing agreements with the proposed international partner(s).

2 Submit the draft agreement proposal form to Global Affairs using the International Agreement Proposal Form.

UC Davis agreement templates are available at globalaffairs.ucdavis.edu/partnerships/agreements.

Global Affairs will respond to your submission within 10 days.

3 Global Affairs reviews the draft agreement, then returns it to the UC Davis agreement sponsor.

The UC Davis agreement sponsor shares the draft agreement with the collaborating institution.

Any changes to the agreement will be clearly marked and must be approved by Global Affairs before signing.

4 Following approval of the draft, the institutional authorities named in the agreement print and sign the agreement.

(Note: faculty have not been delegated the authority to sign international agreements.) UC Davis and the partner institution will each keep a fully executed copy of the agreement.

5 Schools, colleges, departments, centers, and others executing international agreements that fall under these procedures are responsible for coordinating with Global Affairs to ensure Global Affairs has either a copy or original of the sponsoring agreement. Send copies of fully executed agreements to Global Affairs.

Global Affairs will add the document to the central agreements database.

This step-by-step process is designed for faculty members interested in embarking on a collaboration with an international university partner, which DOES NOT involve the commitment of university resources or binding contract provisions for purposes of protecting or utilizing intellectual property.

For additional information and more complete guidance, visit globalaffairs.ucdavis.edu/partnerships/agreements to read the Procedures for International Agreements reviewed by the UC Davis Academic Senate.

Source: University of California, Davis Global Affairs.

Step 1. Contact Global Affairs

The UC Davis international agreements process anticipates two ways in which an international agreement can be initiated: via UC Davis faculty or via external institutions.

When a faculty member requests the formation of an international agreement, Global Affairs helps ensure that the individual is setting up the collaboration in a way that supports the intended objectives and activities of the faculty, while also limiting potential legal and reputational liabilities for the university.

Often, external institutions approach UC Davis for international agreements because they are seeking to initiate or formalize collaborative activities. Institutions may also use international agreements to build their own research capabilities in particular areas or to develop mobility programs by partnering with UC Davis. More recently, other entities, including funding bodies, NGOs, governmental bodies, and industry partners, approach Global Affairs directly to inquire about the possibility for collaboration and agreements.

Regardless of how the request originates, a central requirement of the international agreements process is that there must be both a UC Davis faculty champion and a champion from the partnering institution(s) at the inception of each agreement. Global Affairs will not approve or sign international agreements unless academic faculty champions are clearly identified. The identification of specific faculty champions promotes accountability for the development and progress of the partnership and is also necessary because of the shared governance structure at UC Davis.

Faculty leadership is a central part of UC Davis's institutional culture. The identification of specific faculty champions is not intended to limit the scope of the activities. For example, a faculty member from the School of Engineering may be the faculty champion of an agreement, but the partnership may evolve to include joint activities and faculty involvement across other schools and colleges. However, the initial UC Davis faculty champion is responsible for helping to coordinate reporting on any activities that are undertaken under the auspices of the agreement.

Step 2. Submit a Proposal Form

Whether the initial request for an agreement comes from an internal or external source, a proposal form is required to initiate the agreement process. If the request is external, Global Affairs will reach out to UC Davis faculty members who have ties to that particular institution or the indicated disciplines to see if there is interest in the partnership and to identify a faculty champion. The UC Davis faculty champion prepares and submits the proposal form to Global Affairs.

The form is structured to help faculty articulate immediate goals and tasks for the particular collaboration and identify potential areas for exploration as the partnership develops over time. First, the form asks the faculty champion to identify and provide contact information for the faculty champions of both institutions, along with points of contact at both institutions if these are different. Second, it asks whether the proposed agreement is new or is a renewal of an earlier agreement, and what partnership activities have been completed and are planned. Finally, the form requests a justification for the creation of the agreement: How will it help the individual collaboration? How will it help the university? These questions are intended to elicit thoughtful partnerships and stimulate specific activities.

Signatures on the proposal form may include department heads, associate deans, or unit heads. These signatures ensure transparency with relevant stakeholders and support schools and colleges in monitoring partnerships in their units. The Dean's Office is the final signature required on the form before it is returned to Global Affairs.

Step 3. Review the Proposed Partner and Agreement

Global Affairs examines the proposed agreement along the following fronts:

- Who? Is this an institution that UC Davis wants to partner with? Considerations here include how a collaboration may help move UC Davis's research and pedagogic agendas forward. An additional factor is whether the institution complies with applicable laws and University of California policies regarding international activities. Entity checks are conducted, via software like Visual Compliance, within Global Affairs in consultation with the Office of Research Compliance and Integrity. This screening is one way to identify partnerships that may be high risk to the institution prior to a partnership reaching a more developed state.

- What? Is the proposed agreement advancing UC Davis's mission, values, and strategic priorities?

- When? Is the relationship advanced enough to enter an agreement? Are faculty champions identified on both sides? Is there a clear focus to the intended collaboration? Are there other factors that affect the timing for an agreement with this institution?

- How? What types of collaborations are intended? Is an agreement needed or desired, and if so, what type of agreement is needed? The UC Davis basic agreement template, called the Agreement of Cooperation (AOC), indicates a general intent to partner with another institution. The AOC may reference potential types of collaborations such as exploratory workshops, one-off short-term visits, and the like. Working agreements build on AOCs and may be titled with various names, including Memorandum of Understanding (MOU). Working agreements include further details about a collaboration, such as specific mobility programs or research projects. The same agreement process is used to develop and finalize working agreements. They may be developed simultaneously with an AOC or at a later date.

These questions often require further conversations with the faculty champions and, at times, revisions of the proposal forms. Proposal forms, and the information they contain, are stored within Global Affairs and linked securely to the Global Connections database (globalaffairs.ucdavis.edu/data).

AGREEMENT TEMPLATES AND LANGUAGE

UC Davis has developed a set of template international agreements, in consultation with Campus Counsel, and strongly encourages its faculty and staff to utilize the approved language. Templates are useful for the university in a number of ways:

- They simplify the complexity of drafting agreements on a case-by-case basis;

- They streamline the process for legal review and approval of agreements;

- They facilitate the negotiation of language with partner institutions by articulating institutional preferences and requirements up front; and

- They support more consistency in the international agreements that are being implemented across campus.

Still, UC Davis recognizes that there are cases when the templates are not used—often because the partner institution proposes its own agreement language. UC Davis approaches international agreements with the flexibility to negotiate specific language as needed. However, when the templates are not used, the process for finalizing the language and approving the agreement can become lengthy because Campus Counsel must provide a legal review. Back-and-forth negotiation can take a number of weeks or even months to complete. The time duration that may be involved when text needs to be drafted, negotiated, and redrafted can vary significantly. Global Affairs communicates regularly with the UC Davis faculty and staff involved in the agreement as to where the agreement stands.

Generally, the international agreements being managed and processed by Global Affairs are nonbinding. It is the content of the agreement, rather than the name (e.g., Memorandum of Understanding, Agreement of Cooperation) that controls whether it is considered binding. Thus, it is important to avoid any confusion with language that appears to create specific legal obligations (see table 1). For example, UC Davis avoids words such as "shall" in favor of less obligatory words such as "may."

Table 1. Language of Agreements

Table 1 was adapted from a guidance on MOUs that was jointly developed by Global Affairs and the Office of Research at UC Davis. It lists words and phrases that should be avoided in a nonbinding international agreement. Instead, the alternative words provided can help avoid negative legal implications.

Do Not Use	Use Instead
Shall	Will
Enter into force	Come into effect
Continue in force	Remain in effect
Terms/Conditions	Provisions

Use Discouraged	Use Instead
Agree	Concur
Agreements/Undertakings	Arrangements/Understandings
Undertakes	Intends
Agree(s) to	Will
Party/Parties	Participant(s)
To be entitled to	Enjoy
Commitments	Arrangements
Obligations	Responsibilities
Constitute an obligation	Continue to apply
Rights	Benefits

Source: University of California, Davis Office of Research and Global Affairs (2014).

There are some types of provisions that are common in agreements and, depending on the wording, can have implications for how potential disagreements between the institution and partner are resolved. These provisions often require further negotiation, as institutions have varying preferences regarding risk tolerance. For UC Davis, when a partner institution makes changes to the approved templates in these areas, Global Affairs coordinates with Campus Counsel to mitigate risk and anticipate possible misunderstandings with the partner institution, even for agreements that may be considered nonbinding. These may include:

- Choice of law: provision specifying the governing jurisdiction over disputes arising from or relating to this agreement (e.g., U.S. law, French law, etc.).

- Confidentiality: provision stipulating disclosure to third parties and the authorization that is required.

- Indemnification: provision regarding reimbursement in case of an anticipated loss; compensation for specific circumstances.

- Intellectual property: provision on the ownership of related intellectual property.

- Nonbinding clause: articulates that the agreement is not legally binding and parties are not legally obligated to carry out its terms.

- Prevailing language: provision that addresses which language will prevail (e.g., English) if a conflict between the two languages arises.

- Publication: provision that addresses the right to publish or otherwise make public the agreement or the data that are collected as part of the agreement.

- Termination clause: provision allowing the agreement to be terminated under certain circumstances.

- Use of name: provision that articulates when one party can use the other party's name in publicity or for other purposes.

Working agreements, which provide further detail about planned collaborations, may be developed simultaneously with an AOC or at a later date. UC Davis has developed templates for working agreements, including for mobility and research projects that are not connected to a specific external funding source (globalaffairs.ucdavis.edu/partnerships/agreements/guidelines). Faculty champions for these other agreements may be the same as those of the AOC or may, in fact, come from other disciplines or schools and colleges. If it is the latter, discussions with all the individuals and units involved are important to ensure that collaborations with the other institution are complementary within UC Davis. In all cases of international agreements, Global Affairs is meant to be a repository of knowledge that the agreement exists.

The way that agreement negotiation is handled depends on the institution's level of risk tolerance and the level of flexibility that the institution allows in negotiating or making changes to templates and standard language. It is worth noting that, in some cases, the negotiation may not lead to a satisfactory solution and, in those cases, it may not be possible to complete an international agreement. This does not necessarily mean that collaboration cannot happen, but it may limit the extent of that collaboration.

CAMPUS COORDINATION

In order to ensure that the agreements process runs smoothly, it is vital to create effective lines of communication with a number of offices on campus.

Developing and raising awareness about the international agreements process is a critical step, but it is not sufficient. Even when the process is clearly delineated, campus constituents, especially those who do not have significant experience with international agreements, need support and guidance. This is often time-consuming but also a critical aspect of building awareness and norms to support international engagement.

Global Affairs frequently acts as the conduit routing agreements to other places involved in any individual agreement. It is important to designate a central office to receive inquiries and manage the steps to track international agreements. For UC Davis, Campus Counsel and the Office of Research also play central roles in the process. Global Affairs coordinates constantly with Campus Counsel, especially when negotiation is required with the other institution. A consistent, working-level channel between Global Affairs and Campus Counsel has been essential to ensuring that final agreements reflect the principles and legal requirements of the campus.

UC Davis shares the responsibility for shepherding nonbinding research agreements with the Office of Research. Weekly conversations about agreements in progress and the placement of signing authority for new agreements between the two offices have created a more streamlined process for the faculty, deans, and staff who are involved.

Step 4. Finalize and Sign the Agreement

After the text is negotiated, approved by Campus Counsel, and agreed upon by the other institution, the appropriate authorities must sign the document to bring it into effect.

DELEGATED AUTHORITY

UC Davis has multiple delegated authorities, or designated positions that are permitted to sign on behalf of the university. During the APWG process, it was decided that it would be appropriate to develop a delegation of authority for international agreements. The delegation authority provided that AOCs (general nonbinding international agreements) could be signed by either the chancellor or the vice provost and associate chancellor, Global Affairs, either of whom has the ability to delegate another person to sign in appropriate circumstances. The delegation of authority decisions was designed to retain the existing oversight role of the deans and the Office of Research, amongst others, for collaborations that are pertinent to their units, but also to institutionalize the role of Global Affairs as the central repository for international relationships.

Nonbinding AOCs that are facilitated by Global Affairs and signed by the vice provost and associate chancellor, Global Affairs, may be followed by more specific agreements that can be either nonbinding or binding. These may include provisions relating to funding, intellectual property, or publication rights. For these follow-up agreements, other units may retain certain types of signing authority, and it falls to Global Affairs to identify the appropriate authority. However, a signed copy of every international agreement should be provided to Global Affairs.

UC Davis policy requires an original signature from the UC Davis signatories to execute an international agreement. This ensures that the appropriate individuals and offices at UC Davis have reviewed and approved the final text of the agreement. In many other institutions, electronic signatures are permitted for executing international agreements.

Along with a filed hard copy of the agreement, Global Affairs documents international agreements in an agreements database. Data on the agreement, faculty champions, points of contact, and dates in effect are collected, as is information from the proposal form documenting the aims of the collaboration. Global Affairs utilizes this information to track the history of partnerships by country and institution. Keeping in mind the necessities of the General Data Protection Regulation (GDPR), components of the information in the database, such as the name of the collaborating institution, the UC Davis faculty champion, and the expiry date, form the public-facing side of the database (globalaffairs.ucdavis.edu/data).

Step 5. Track and Monitor Activities and Facilitate Further Collaboration

An agreement doesn't end with the signing—indeed, it has only just begun. For the international agreements process to work smoothly and to cultivate active relationships that forward the UC Davis strategic agenda, monitoring and tracking the development of individual agreements is important.

REPORTING AND MONITORING PROGRESS

Reports are built into the agreement process at both the midterm point (normally after 2 years) and final stages. A final report is requested prior to renewal of an agreement. The report documents the activities undertaken under the aegis of the agreement. This can be as simple as a series of bullet points indicating what happened over time and may include the ways in which an AOC has blossomed into a multilayered series of agreements as the collaboration has grown. The report is submitted by the faculty champion, but for those that have generated a number of subsequent working agreements, information may come from a number of different places. With the new UC Davis Global Connections database (globalaffairs.ucdavis.edu/data), Global Affairs has refined the ways to link and track agreements from the same institution, which will assist in monitoring the depth of an individual partnership and identifying those promising partnerships that might need further facilitation to grow.

Conclusion

International agreement processes should be flexible to accommodate changes in policy and structure within the institution. Raising awareness and changing norms about the process and requirements can take significant time and effort. Institutions and internal stakeholders can be resistant to changing established and ingrained behaviors. Clear process and guidelines, including templates and reporting mechanisms, provide consistency in an institution and support the sustainability of partnerships and collaborations.

At UC Davis, Global Affairs, together with campus partners, continues to review and revise procedures based on what is working (and not working). Such revision may comprise modifications of agreement templates, improvements in data collection, and changes to facilitate campus coordination on international agreements. Close partners that may be involved in the review process include the Office of Research and Campus Counsel. UC Davis also utilizes systemwide resources supported by the Office of the President, the UC Global Operations website, and discussion groups across the international offices in the UC system.

As the international agreement process becomes socialized on the campus, units now turn to Global Affairs to manage general nonbinding international agreements that had previously come to them. The institutionalization of Global Affairs's management and oversight of international agreements will enable UC Davis to increase the depth and quality of its international collaborations.

Reference

University of California, Davis Office of Research and Global Affairs. 2014. *International Memorandum of Understanding (MOU) Basic Guide*. Davis, California: University of California, Davis. https://research.ucdavis.edu/wp-content/uploads/UC-Davis-Intl-MOU-Basic-Guide.pdf.

8

International Partnerships Assessment Rating Index
A CASE STUDY FROM UNIVERSITY OF CALGARY

*Janaka Y. Ruwanpura, Andrea Delgado Morrow, Savera Hayat-Dade,
Colleen Packer, and Scott Vu*

A core element of university work and advancement in internationalization involves building, cultivating, and maintaining relationships with other universities that help to both expand networks and increase impact. All universities have a certain number of these international partnerships in place, but are the universities strategically evaluating and prioritizing those connections that best meet their objectives?

This chapter showcases the International Partnership Assessment Rating Index (IPARI), a unique ranking system developed by the University of Calgary (UCalgary) to assess and evaluate existing university partnerships. Ensuring that UCalgary has agreements that align with its international goals and visions is key to advancing its institutional international strategy. Creating a more strategic approach to managing and evaluating agreements was necessary to ensure the effectiveness and efficiency of the investment of people, time, and funding to support the vision of the internationalization of the institute.

International Strategy

In 2012, the University of Calgary launched a new International Strategy (UCalgary 2012; Marshall and Ruwanpura 2019). The strategy outlined four strategic goals:

1. Diversity: Increase the diversity of UCalgary's campus communities.

2. Cross-Cultural Competencies: Improve the global and cross-cultural competencies within the campus communities.

3. Partnerships: Enhance opportunities for international collaborations and partnerships in research and education.

4. International development: Leverage areas of expertise to engage in international development.

Each of these goals involves a direction toward developing, maintaining, and sustaining partnerships around the world to advance the university's position as an intellectual, social, and cultural hub for academics and research.

One of the biggest challenges was to determine the status of UCalgary's partnerships, regardless the existence of a formal agreement between the partners. As one of Canada's top comprehensive research universities, UCalgary had hundreds of active institutional agreements managed by the university's international office. These agreements ranged from memoranda of understanding (MOUs) to specific or supplemental agreements. Ensuring that all agreements were monitored, reviewed, and evaluated on a frequent basis, and assessing the nature of each relationship and status of the agreements also created challenges for the international office.

Purpose of IPARI

No matter the type or structure of the university, the senior international officer (SIO) and the members of the international office need to understand the status of each university partnership and assess them on a regular basis. This analysis allows the key stakeholders to connect with the faculties, schools, and units of the home university to develop meaningful university partnerships.

At UCalgary, the need for an assessment criterion and model was identified by the SIO and staff of the international office, which led to the development of IPARI.

The main purposes of IPARI are to:

• Assess existing university partnerships. Often, universities have multiple agreements with many partner universities. These agreements could function at an institutional level or focus specifically on a faculty, department, or school. At UCalgary, it was often challenging for the international office to understand and track the actual results of an agreement. Thus, finding a way to understand and assess active agreements on an annual basis became one of the main goals for IPARI.

- Identify top partner universities in each country. It was important to understand the depth and breadth of each partnership and to take the time to determine the partner university's strongest and most consistent international activities and priorities. By being able to identify the top partner universities (i.e., most active partners with many projects that mutually benefit both the home and partner universities), it becomes easier to identify strategic partners and projects that could enhance internationalization.

- Re-engage partners. Universities should review the agreements that have lapsed or been curtailed and seek to understand the reasons behind these changes. There are many reasons and factors that can contribute to an unsuccessful agreement. For example, faculty members who were once the champions of the partnership move or retire; political, social, or economic changes impact the level of engagement; or institutional priorities or programs change the nature of the partnership.

- Identify inactive partners. Many universities have hundreds of agreements that developed over the years, but a large number of universities struggle to understand how many of these arrangements produce meaningful activity. From UCalgary's experience, trying to manage and analyze these agreements to ensure they align with the international strategy and its goals was a challenge. A criterion was needed to understand partnerships through qualitative and quantitative lenses and determine whether to eliminate those that did not support the intended internationalization or institutional strategies and goals. Focusing on just the active partners helps to reserve energies and resources and contributes toward meeting institutional goals.

Rationale and Process for Developing IPARI

International partnerships should be focused, with clearly defined objectives that relate to the broader strategic goals while leveraging existing resources and strengths. It is important that partnerships be developed by considering the mutual benefits to the partners and ensuring they are sustainable and multi-faceted. This involves reinforced synergies among multiple points of contact. Concurrently, the university may want to limit the number of international projects and partnerships in place so that they can be sustained given the available resources.

UCalgary's IPARI helps to assess the university's existing and potential partnerships under the university's larger strategies and goals. There are two main components of IPARI: qualitative and quantitative. The qualitative component comprises the principles of internationalization. The quantitative component constitutes the criteria and scoring system.

Qualitative

UCalgary's international office uses the following principles to develop its internationalization plan and manage its partnerships:

- Strategy. It may be important for the university to strategically work with universities and organizations that are highly ranked internationally within their geographic area or within specific fields of strategic interest. Exceptions are made when the partnership accomplishes specific educational, research, or service objectives that relate to unique circumstances at the potential partner institution.

- Entrepreneurism. The university must encourage and facilitate international interactions at the faculty and student levels. Faculty members should strive to maintain networks of international collaborators.

- Structure. The university must have an effective organizational structure at the institutional level to support the internationalization plan, as well as a visionary and effective executive and senior leadership.

- Incentives. Sustaining international activities must involve creating and maintaining incentive structures at the faculty level that will drive achievement of the goals of the internationalization plan.

- Capacity building. As unique repositories of knowledge, universities must leverage their expertise to contribute to civil society and capacity development globally.

- Risk management. The operation of all international activities must proceed within an enterprise-wide risk management framework that includes reputational and financial risk assessment. The safety and security of students, faculty, and staff is paramount.

- Sustainability. The value of international initiatives and activities must be assessed relative to their overall impact. Once partnerships are established, technology-enabled solutions to maintain activities should be explored whenever possible.

Quantitative

To examine the quantitative nature of partnerships, UCalgary's international office created a committee to review various types of agreements and projects with partner universities. An analysis of existing activities and agreements was conducted by utilizing an internally developed international relations management database system. Extensive conversations were held around how the points should be allocated. Three broad categories were defined:

- Academic programs and collaboration. These include activities related to the delivery of academic programs, such as dual degrees, training programs, articulation agreements, and international development programs.

- Mobility programs. These include activities and projects related to the mobility of students, staff, and faculty, such as exchange programs, faculty-led group study programs, internships, volunteer activities, etc.

- Research collaborations and impact. These include both the activities and projects related to research collaborations between the home university and the partner university as well as the academic publications coauthored by personnel from the home university and the partner university.

To ensure that each category was explored and further analyzed, the vice provost international (VPI), in essence the SIO at UCalgary, established three subcommittees that included representation from different units within the international office. The objectives for each subcommittee included:

1. Identify all activities, projects, and programs under each heading and create an assessment criterion; and

2. Determine how those identified criteria can be assessed using a scoring system.

It took about 6 months for the subcommittees to complete the objectives. When the VPI and the subcommittees finalized the criteria and the scoring system, the draft IPARI was presented to the Associate Deans Council International (Marshall and Ruwanpura 2019), Deans Council, the provost, and the vice president (research) for their comments and feedback.

Criteria for IPARI

The finalized IPARI model includes three broad categories, with a total possible score of 30 points (see figure 1).

Academic Programs and Collaborations

The academic programs and collaborations category includes the following assessed subcategories:

- Articulation programs. In 2014, UCalgary launched a number of international collaborative degree programs. These programs allow international students to earn two degrees: one from their home university and one from UCalgary. Similarly, UCalgary has dual-degree programs at the master's level, such as 1+1 programs. UCalgary has developed several partnerships for these international collaborative degree programs and is in the process of finalizing additional agreements.

Figure 1. IPARI Model

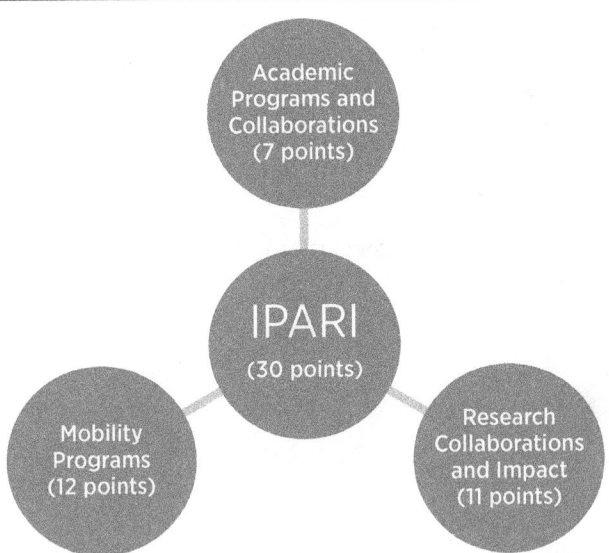

Source: UC International.

- PhD cotutelle programs. A "cotutelle" is a PhD program in which a doctoral candidate is jointly enrolled at two universities and spends time at each university. The cotutelle PhD candidate is jointly supervised by academic faculty members at each university and, upon successful completion of the program, graduates from both universities with a doctor of philosophy and receives two degree parchments. UCalgary currently has 23 partnerships under this arrangement.

- Training programs. Some of UCalgary's partnerships include customized training programs for students or academic staff of partner universities. These programs range from upgrading the skills of pipeline engineers from Mexico to giving Chinese social work students a firsthand Canadian perspective.

- Special projects. In addition to some of the traditional partnerships, UCalgary has a variety of other partnerships. These partnerships include having a satellite office at a partner university (e.g., the UCalgary office at the National Autonomous University of Mexico in Mexico City), working with a partner university on an international development project (e.g., Aga Khan University), and having partner universities that are members of an international university consortium (e.g., the Worldwide Energy University Network).

Figure 2 depicts the criteria and scoring system for the academic programs and collaborations category.

Figure 2. Criteria and Scoring System for Academic Programs and Collaborations

Criteria	Points Assigned	
Annual # of Students – Active Articulation Agreements (2+2/3+2, dual degrees, 1+1)	1 to 5 = 1 6 to 10 = 2 10+ = 3	
Cotutelle (student participation in past 3 years)	Maximum = 2 (up to 3 students = 1, otherwise 2)	
Training/Professional Programs (students in past 3 years)	Maximum = 1	
Engaged for Special Projects (ex: a program at host university for international development, UCalgary Office, network)	Yes = 1	

Source: UC International.

- Articulation programs. To evaluate articulation programs, points are assigned based on a scale that reflects the number of students enrolled from each partner university. The scale assigns 1 point to a partner university that has one to five students enrolled in the program, 2 points to a partner university that has six to 10 students enrolled, and 3 points to a partner university that has more than 10 students enrolled.

- PhD cotutelle programs. The scale assigns a maximum of 2 points if there are more than three PhD students enrolled between the home university and the partner university. If the number of PhD students is fewer than three, but at least one, the partner university receives 1 point.

- Training programs. Given that training programs and their frequency change throughout the years, the scale assigns a maximum of 1 point to the partner university if UCalgary offers a training program in the assessed year.

- Special projects. Similar to the infrequency of training program, special projects are often sporadic. If a special project is in place during the year of assessment, the scale assigns 1 point to the partner university.

Mobility Programs

The mobility programs category includes three subcategories: student exchanges, staff exchanges, and other niche collaborations related to mobility purposes. Approximately 1,200 UCalgary students gain a valuable international learning experience every year through mobility programs. UCalgary has 158 mobility-related agreements with 140 partner universities in 41 countries. Figure 3 depicts the criteria and scoring system for the mobility programs category.

Figure 3. Criteria and Scoring System for Mobility Programs

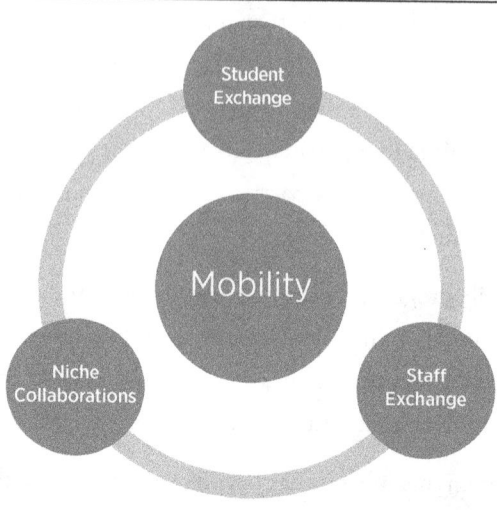

Criteria	Points Assigned	
Number of Exchange Students Total In and Out (average for the last 3 years)	1 to 4	= 1
	5 to 8	= 2
	8+	= 3
Balance of Exchange Students (average for the last 3 years)	Balanced	= 1
	Not Balanced	= 0
Scope of Exchange (general or more than 1 faculty/department specific)	Faculty/Dept.	= 1
	General	= 2
Niche Collaboration (group study program [GSP] site, internship, etc.)	Maximum	= 4
	GSP (site = 1, more than 15 UC students = 1, includes students from host = 1), Internship	= 1
Active Faculty/Staff Exchange	Yes	= 1
Over 10 Years of Active Exchange Agreement	Yes	= 1

Source: UC International.

- Student exchanges. A student exchange agreement allows students to spend a semester or year studying at a partner university while continuing to pay tuition to the home university. An average of the total number of exchange students (both incoming and outgoing) from the last 3 years was calculated for each partner university, and a scale system was created to determine point allocations. The scale assigns 1 point to a partner university that exchanges one to four students, 2 points to a partner university that exchanges five to eight students, and 3 points to a partner university that exchanges more than eight students. UCalgary added three conditions for student exchanges and assigned scores accordingly:

- Exchange agreements work on the premise that there is a balance in the number of incoming and outgoing students over the course of the agreement. If there is a reasonable balance (the international office assigned a threshold balance of zero to three students) maintained between the home and partner universities, 1 additional point is awarded.

- If the scope of the exchange agreement includes more than one academic faculty member, 2 additional points are awarded. If the exchange is limited to only one faculty member, only 1 additional point is awarded to recognize the existence of the exchange program.

- Considering the qualitative criterion principle of "sustainability," 1 additional point is awarded if the exchange program has been successfully maintained for more than 10 years.

- Faculty and staff exchanges. The scale assigns 1 point in recognition of the existence of a formal staff exchange program between the home and partner universities.

- Niche collaborations. In addition to traditional exchanges, there are many other ways for students to gain international learning experiences. For example, UCalgary includes:

  - Credit programs such as exchanges, faculty-led group study programs, co-operative education/internship/practicums, research activity abroad, independent studies, etc. It can also be a credit program from another university undertaken on a letter of permission.

– Noncredit programs and activities that are organized and/or supported by UCalgary, which could include financial support, staff and faculty administrative support, and guidance by the relevant faculties and the international office. Examples include UCalgary's international service-learning programs.

For international learning experiences, a maximum of 4 points can be assigned based on the following factors:

- The scale assigns 1 point if the home university organizes a faculty-led group study program involving students in coordination with the partner university.

- The scale assigns 1 point if the program has more than 15 students from the home university.

- The scale assigns 1 point if the program includes collaboration with students from the partner university.

- The scale assigns 1 point if the home or the partner university has engaged in research internships at the undergraduate level.

Research Collaborations and Impact

This category assesses research collaborations and impact in terms of publications between the home and partner universities. It has four subcategories. Figure 4 depicts the criteria and scoring system for the research collaborations and impact category.

- Special agreements. This subcategory recognizes the existence of any formal research agreements between the home and partner universities. The scale currently assigns 1 point for a partner university that has at least one research agreement. International office staff members are exploring a scaled point system based on the number of agreements in the future.

Figure 4. Criteria and Scoring System for Research Collaborations and Impact

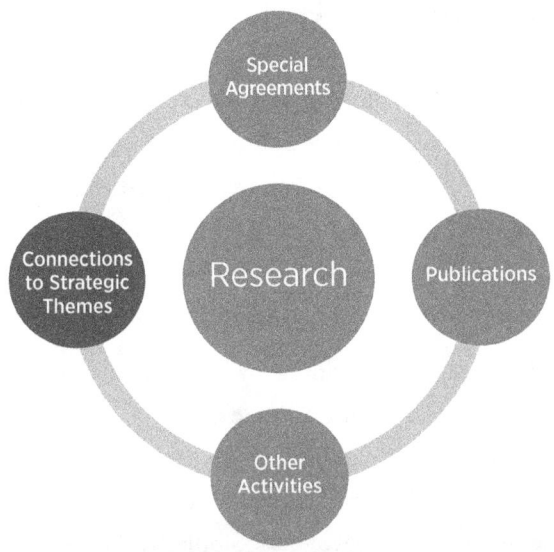

Criteria	Points Assigned	
Specific Research Agreement	Yes	= 1
Research/Commercialization Activity (identify specific activity, collaboration, joint supervision, participation in thesis examination, etc.)	Maximum	= 1
Joint Publications (in past 3 years) – based on SCOPUS – Total	1 to 25	= 1
	26 to 50	= 2
	50+	= 3
Distribution Publications in Disciplines (SCOPUS – range of faculties)	1 to 3 faculties	= 1
	4 to 6 faculties	= 2
	7+ faculties	= 3
Active Connections/Projects to Research Themes	Maximum	= 3

Source: UC International.

- Publications. Research publications coauthored by academics and students from the home and partner universities are tracked using Elsevier's Scopus, the largest abstract and citation database of peer-reviewed literature. International office staff developed a macro-based computer template using Microsoft Excel to track·these publications with ease. The publications are counted as an average for the last 3 years. The scale assigns 1 point for up to 25 publications, 2 points for 26 to 50 publications, and 3 points for more than 50 publications.

Staff in the international office also look at the distribution of publications in terms of scope and faculties. If the publications represent up to three faculties at the partner (with corresponding home faculties), 1 additional point is awarded. Similarly, representation of four to six faculty is awarded 2 points, and representation of 7+ faculty is awarded 3 points. It is important to note that there are limitations in publication search engines related to areas such as the performing and visual arts and humanities. The international office is planning further research to include publications in these areas in the future.

- Other activities. Other activities may be related to research and commercialization between the home and partner universities. Some partners do not have formal PhD cotutelle programs; however, they have involved home faculty in research projects of PhD students at the partner university, or vice versa. Similarly, there may be research commercialization projects between the home and partner universities that are assigned a maximum of 1 point.

- Connection to research themes. The purpose of this subcategory is to determine the existence of research projects jointly managed by academics from the home and the partner universities. This is often more difficult to identify, therefore, research dollars (as an average per year during the last 3 years) was added as a criterion to recognize the value of research partnerships.

  - The scale assigns 1 point for research dollars of up to $50,000.
  - The scale assigns 2 points for research dollars between $50,000 and $250,000.
  - The scale assigns 3 points for research dollars beyond $250,000.

By considering all three categories of IPARI—academic programs and collaborations, mobility programs, and research collaborations and impact—the maximum total score is 30 points (see figure 1). While designed for UCalgary, many SIOs and partnership managers at other institutions can adapt the model to their needs.

Results of IPARI

In addition to the four goals outlined in its International Strategy, UCalgary identified a regional/country framework to focus the university's international activities (Marshall and Ruwanpura 2019). To do so, UCalgary cross-referenced projects, travel, student recruitment, and research partnerships within identified geographic concentrations. This analysis yielded countries/regions of emphasis and countries/regions of interest.

Countries and regions of emphasis represent areas where there are already ongoing institutional relationships, strong ties to the university's academic and research priority areas, and potential connections to industry in both Calgary and in the country or region of emphasis. The university has also considered areas where existing relationships or partnerships are less well established but where compelling opportunities exist to further enhance internationalization activities. In addition, the analysis considers whether strong diasporic or immigrant populations from each of these countries and regions exist in Calgary (Marshall and Ruwanpura 2019).

Six countries of emphasis were identified: China, Germany, Mexico, Tanzania, the Middle East and the United States. The 13 countries of interest include Australia, Brazil, France, India, Japan, Malaysia, Norway, Singapore, South Korea, Spain, Thailand, United Kingdom, and Vietnam. Figure 5 shows the IPARI analysis for these six countries of emphasis and 13 countries of interest.

According to the analysis (see figure 5):

- In 2017–18, UCalgary had 150 active partnerships with partner universities in 19 countries of emphasis and interest:

  - 7 partner universities include all three categories: academic programs and collaborations, mobility, and research collaborations and impact.

  - 13 of them are academic programs and collaborations and research collaborations and impact only.

  - 65 of them are mobility and research collaborations and impact only.

  - 18 of them are mobility only.

  - 37 of them are research collaborations and impact only.

- There were also 14 inactive partnerships.

Figure 5. IPARI Analysis for UCalgary's Countries of Emphasis and Interest

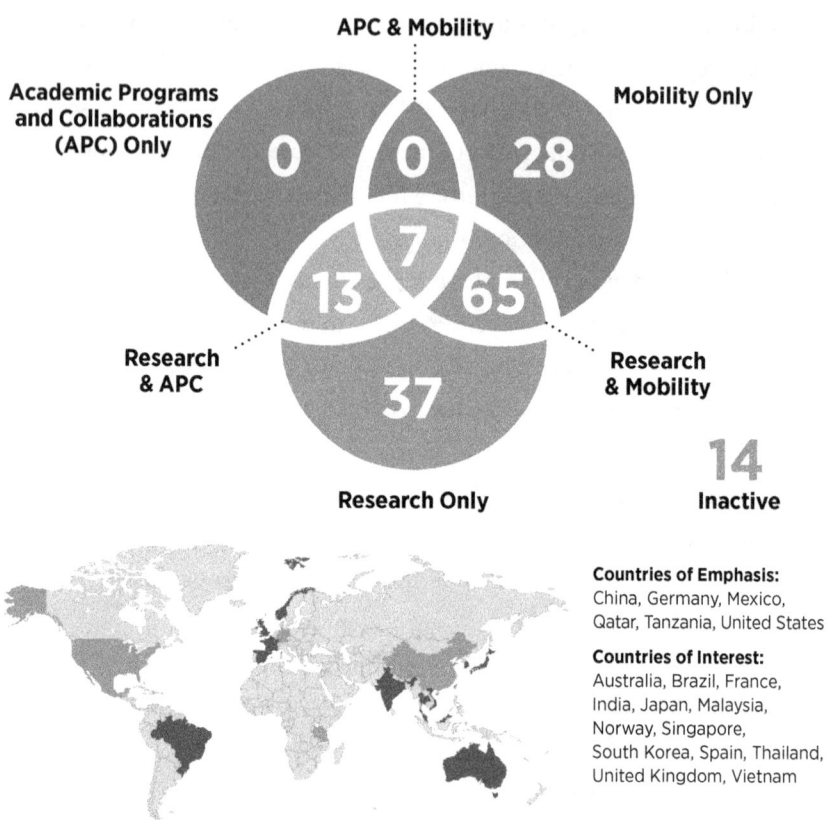

APC & Mobility

Academic Programs and Collaborations (APC) Only

Mobility Only

0   0   28

7

13   65

Research & APC

Research & Mobility

37

14

Research Only   **Inactive**

Countries of Emphasis:
China, Germany, Mexico, Qatar, Tanzania, United States

Countries of Interest:
Australia, Brazil, France, India, Japan, Malaysia, Norway, Singapore, South Korea, Spain, Thailand, United Kingdom, Vietnam

Source: UC International Feb. 16, 2018.
Note: Based on six countries of emphasis and 13 countries of interest.

In addition to analyzing UCalgary's countries of emphasis and interest, an IPARI analysis was conducted for each region and, in some instances, country. It can also be used to identify the top university partners for each country or region, or top partners overall in any one of the three categories (academic programs and collaborations, mobility, and research collaborations and impact). Figure 6 shows the country representation of UCalgary's top 10 partner institutions covering all three categories. IPARI analyses can also show the country representation of the top 10 partners for each separate category.

Figure 6. Country Representation of the Top 10 Partner Universities Covering All Three Categories

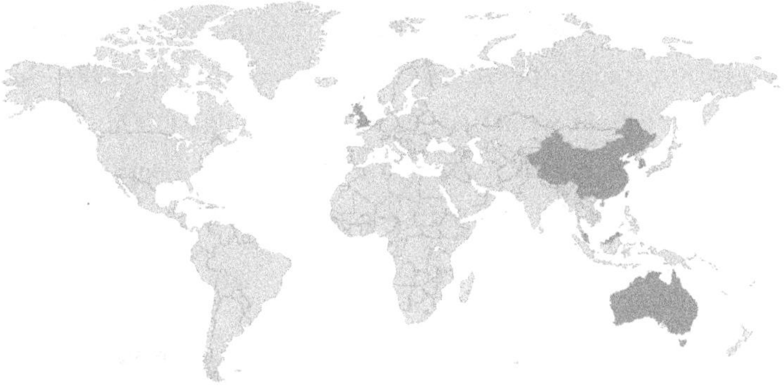

Rank	Country
1	China
2	Australia
3	Australia
4	Australia
5	Hong Kong
6	Singapore
7	Singapore
8	England
9	Australia
10	Korea

Source: UC International.

Limitations of the Methodology

There are some limitations to the methodology and analysis of IPARI. First, the points assigned for each category, including the subcategories, were assigned based on the consensus of the team that developed IPARI. It is also important to note that the committee that created the ranking index was internal. Although there are advantages to having those who are directly involved with international activities creating the rankings, there could have been unintentional biases. During the process, initial literature was reviewed; however, a thorough research project would enhance the current weights for each subcategory. UCalgary is planning on initiating a comprehensive research project in the near future.

The second limitation is that the current methodology requires there to be at least one active agreement or MOU in place in order to count and recognize the partnership. However, it was noted that the methodology for measuring the research collaborations and impact category counts publications between UCalgary and a partner institution only if there is some type of agreement (academic, mobility, or research) in place, not necessarily a research agreement.

When the Scopus publications between UCalgary and other universities were analyzed, it was discovered that there were many universities with which UCalgary copublishes but does not have formal partnerships. For example, figures 7 and 8 show the countries of the top 10 universities for medical and nonmedical coauthored publications. The volume of coauthored publications is relatively high in medical publications (see figure 7) due to clinical studies; however, only two of the 10 universities have any type of formal agreement with UCalgary. In nonmedical publications, only six of the 10 universities (see figure 8) have any type of formal agreement with UCalgary. The university is working on identifying these partners and signing agreements with top coauthor publication universities so that those universities can be counted as formal university partners.

Figure 7. Countries of the Top 10 Universities with the Most Coauthored Medical Publications with UCalgary

Rank	Country
1	USA
2	USA
3	USA
4	USA
5	USA
6	England
7	England
8	USA
9	Australia
10	Australia

Source: UC International.

Figure 8. Countries of the Top 10 Universities with the Most Coauthored Nonmedical Publications with UCalgary

Rank	Country
1	China
2	USA
3	USA
4	USA
5	Hong Kong
6	China
7	USA
8	China
9	England
10	England

Source: UC International.

Benefits and Outcomes

IPARI has helped UCalgary to align its internationalization efforts with larger university goals and visions, providing a snapshot analysis of the status of its international partnerships. Of UCalgary's 405 agreements with 238 universities in 55 countries in place during the 2017–18 academic year, the analysis gave data to indicate the status of each subcategory as well as UCalgary's top partners in each country. IPARI has led to both internal and external benefits.

Internal Benefits and Outcomes

Although UCalgary's International Strategy identified 19 countries of emphasis and interest based on specific criteria (Marshall and Ruwanpura 2019), the IPARI analysis identified stronger partnerships with partner universities in countries beyond those 19. Thirty-five of the 238 universities received the highest ratings for the 2017–18 academic year, including four partner universities in the Netherlands and one partner university from Sweden, which allowed UCalgary's international office to strategically consider those countries when the university renews its international strategy.

Based on the analysis, the international office is better able to align resources (financial, human, and social capital) to achieve UCalgary's research and educational objectives. By identifying the top partners, IPARI helps the international office work with faculties to ensure that internationalization efforts and resources are invested with the right partner institutions to enhance outcomes and sustainability.

UCalgary's international office has been able to increase the effectiveness and accountability of its international efforts by using IPARI. UCalgary is able to make data-driven decisions and can justify the rationale behind renewing or terminating an agreement. IPARI has also helped to mitigate risks. Through the assessment of existing partnerships, the international office has been able to identify and monitor any partnerships that may be at risk. The data have helped to identify strategic partners and potential opportunities to enhance and build on current relationships.

The international office can identify partnerships for further strengthening. There are cases where significant effort has already been invested into developing and implementing a partnership, yet there is still effort required to strengthen the results in terms of IPARI rankings. In such cases, IPARI can help identify these partners so that more concentrated support can be provided to the faculty to move the partnership to the next level.

Finally, IPARI assists in developing partnership implementation plans. Through annual analysis of the data, IPARI can identify partnerships as they move from an early to an intermediate stage. Once those partner universities are identified, targeted partnership implementation plans can be developed in consultation with the international office and related faculties or schools.

External Benefits and Outcomes

Through sharing IPARI data, UCalgary's international partners can learn about their strategic position and try to further align the respective mandates to enhance benefits and outcomes. For example, UCalgary's VPI used a case study to test the validity of the IPARI analysis with the top six partner universities in the United Kingdom. In 2017, the VPI made a strategic visit to the top six partner universities to discuss opportunities to strengthen and build the existing partnerships to a higher strategic level. This has led to further collaboration, such as the exploration of a new three-way collaborative partnership with UCalgary's top partners in China and the United Kingdom. Recognition can lead to further explorations of joint ideas, which further strengthen the partnership by aligning resources, creating synergies, and reaching greater impact.

UCalgary is better able to identify opportunities to enhance relationships. As a result of the above mentioned visit to the United Kingdom, the development offices at both UCalgary and a partner university are exploring a new project to raise scholarship funding from the diasporic communities and corporate sector organizations operating in both cities to enhance mobility programs.

UCalgary's international office is working with a number of faculties to develop synergies and leverage resources to foster strong ties between UCalgary and its top partner university. Recently, the international office and UCalgary's Schulich School of Engineering allocated funding for a group of UCalgary researchers to work with a partner university in Australia. The UCalgary team had visited the partner university the previous summer to hold a workshop with researchers from the partner university and to develop a five-year plan. The reciprocal visit from the partner university was held in 2019 to finalize the plan and work on identified projects. In collaboration with the faculties, UCalgary's international office is exploring other similar activities to enhance strategic partnerships.

Next Steps

Through feedback received from presentations made at international conferences, it became clear that there is currently no model similar to IPARI that assesses university partnerships. Some universities have already shown an active interest in either using IPARI or creating a modified version of IPARI to cater to their own international strategy. For example, one Australian university has invited UCalgary's VPI to present IPARI to its executive leadership team. The Australian university has already sent a delegation to UCalgary to discuss the implement of IPARI. Similarly, the international office has received interest from other universities in Brazil, Canada, the United Kingdom, and the United States.

A prototype of an online portal with data visualization capabilities that will house IPARI has been completed and is moving into the next stage of development. This online portal will ultimately streamline previous processes, generate reports on an annual basis, and share IPARI results with internal stakeholders. Users can upload their datasets, modify the scope, apply a variety of filters to their liking, and generate intuitive graphs that represent the strength of their international partnerships. Currently, users can generate Venn diagrams and grid-style ranking charts, however the plan is to also implement a heat map with a world map overlay. In addition, UCalgary's international office plans to build a stable online version where IPARI can be turned into a product that can be shared with international universities.

Looking into the future, the international office hopes to develop the ability to include other organizations, such as governments, companies, and nongovernmental organizations, in IPARI. Due to the different nature of these organizations and the type of work they do, their assessment must be conducted separately from universities in order to maintain the integrity of IPARI. This will require extensive consultation and stakeholder engagement, similar to the engagement process undergone in the initial development phase of the current IPARI.

Finally, UCalgary is working on initiating a comprehensive research project to review current ranking systems and categories. The university is in discussions with some of its strategic partner institutions about creating working groups to review the ranking system and obtain feedback.

Conclusion

The development of IPARI provides an essential annual assessment of the status of existing university partnerships in the academic, mobility, and research categories. The data reveal where partnerships are at both the faculty and institutional levels. This information allows faculties to identify opportunities to build upon existing partnerships and, in some instances, collaborate with other faculties to further strengthen a partnership.

It is important to note that the compilation of data is always a challenge at large institutions. Datasets range in regard to the time frame in which they were captured, as well as the definition of the data. This is problematic because sometimes data are not consistently available. Coordinating and cross-referencing data is important in ensuring that IPARI results are accurate. A staff member could be responsible for collecting data from campus stakeholders, compiling the data in a format usable to the international office, verifying the data, and conducting the IPARI analysis.

Universities that wish to develop their own IPARI model are strongly encouraged to house IPARI within their international office. Institutions can start by identifying their own institutional priorities for international partnerships. From there, they should seek internal consensus through consultations with key stakeholders from across the institution (i.e., administration, faculties, and business units). A three-category approach may be a good starting point, although it is likely that consultation with stakeholders will result in modifications to the subcategories and point allocations, as the tool is most effective if it is aligned with the specific strategic priorities of the institution.

While the process of developing an IPARI model can take time, it has numerous, long-lasting benefits. Even the consultations and discussions that take place during the development stage will lead to increased awareness and buy-in from the stakeholders involved. IPARI is not only a tool, it is also a way to think about and manage resources and activities related to internalization. The University of Calgary International received two innovation awards for developing IPARI from the Canadian Bureau for International Education (2019) and the Association of International Education Administrators (2020).

Acknowledgments: The authors wish to acknowledge the efforts of the staff of University of Calgary International (UCI) for their work in developing IPARI, including Glynn Hunter, former director of UCI, and Alexa Stollbert, former UCI information officer. The authors also acknowledge the services of Daniel Ernesto Romero Mancia for assisting in developing the prototype of the IPARI online portal.

References

Marshall, Dru, and Janaka Y. Ruwanpura. 2019. "International Strategy Development: University of Calgary Case Study." In *Senior International Officers: Essential Roles and Responsibilities*, ed. David L. Di Maria. Washington, DC: NAFSA: Association of International Educators.

University of Calgary (UCalgary). 2012. *International Strategy*. Calgary, Canada: University of Calgary.

About the Authors

Kiki Caruson is the assistant vice president for research, innovation, and global affairs for the University of South Florida (USF) system. In this capacity, she provides leadership regarding the university's global engagement strategy, including education abroad activities, international research services, and partnership development. Caruson also manages the USF Global Discovery Hub and was the recipient of a Society for Research Administrators International's Big Ideas grant, which funded the development of the Global Research Toolkit. Caruson received her bachelor's degree from Smith College, her master's degree from Johns Hopkins University, and her doctoral degree from the University of Georgia.

Joël A. Gallegos is assistant provost for international programs at the University of North Carolina at Charlotte (UNC Charlotte) where he overseas campuswide internationalization efforts, including education abroad and exchange, international student and scholar services, intensive English language, intercultural outreach, and on-campus internationalization. Previously, Gallegos served as director of education abroad at UNC Charlotte and director of study abroad and instructor of French at the University of Toledo. He holds an MA in French literature from Bowling Green State University. Gallegos serves on the Board of Directors of NAFSA, the Fund for Education Abroad, and the World Affairs Council of Charlotte.

Jane Gatewood serves as vice provost for global engagement at the University of Rochester where she leads and manages initiatives related to the university's global activities. In this role, she oversees the institution's international initiatives, focusing on the identification and development of partnership opportunities in research, teaching, and education. Her administrative experience includes developing complex bi- and multi-lateral international partnerships for research, educational mobility, and economic development across cultures and educational sectors. Gatewood holds a BA from Emory University and a PhD from the University of Georgia. She was a Fulbright-Nehru awardee and an Andrew W. Mellon Fellow at the School of Advanced Study at the University of London.

Savera Hayat-Dade is director of programs and international development at the University of Calgary. With more than 20 years of experience as an international development expert, Hayat-Dade has demonstrated expertise in the areas of evaluation, research, and capacity development. Working for USAID, International Youth Foundation (USA), World Bank, Social Research and Demonstration Corporation (Canada), Aga Khan University, University of Calgary, CANADEM, and Cowater International, she has conducted assessments and developed evaluation frameworks for security, youth employment, education, and governance programs. With an MSc in development management from London School of Economics and Political Science, Hayat-Dade's research interests include social construction and global development.

Chad Hoseth is director of international initiatives at Colorado State University (CSU) where he is responsible for initiatives that help CSU achieve its strategic goals for comprehensive campus internationalization. His focus is on managing special partnerships, supporting faculty and their global interests, and fostering academic and cocurricular opportunities. Hoseth has an MA in international affairs from The George Washington University. He was a Fulbright Scholar on the International Education Administrators Program in Korea, and he is pursuing a PhD in higher education leadership from Colorado State University.

Elizabeth Langridge-Noti has recently returned from living, teaching, and excavating in Greece to take up the position of the director of faculty engagement, global affairs at the University of California, Davis. In her role, Langridge-Noti helps facilitate faculty activity and collaboration on global projects and partnerships, including currently supervising UC Davis's international agreements process. She holds a BA in classical languages from University of California, Berkeley, and an MA and PhD in classical archaeology from Princeton University.

Paul Allen Miller is vice provost and Carolina Distinguished Professor at the University of South Carolina. He has held visiting appointments at the University of the Ruhr (Bochum), the University of Paris 13, and Beijing Language and Cultural University. Miller is currently director of Global Carolina. He holds a PhD in comparative literature from the University of Texas. He has edited 15 volumes of essay and published 80 articles.

Andrea Delgado Morrow is the director, international relations for the University of Calgary's international office, where she and the team are responsible for institutional partnerships and agreements. She has more than 15 years of experience working in post-secondary education. This includes the University of Calgary and her roles as regional manager (Asia-Pacific) and associate faculty member at Royal Roads University and Mount Royal University (faculty of communication). Morrow has served on various committees throughout her career and currently leads the data management group for the Canadian Bureau for International Education's international relations professional learning community. She holds an MA in intercultural and international communication from Royal Roads University.

Colleen Packer has worked in the field of international education for more than 20 years. She is currently the director, international learning programs at University of Calgary International. Packer provides leadership for the university's education abroad programs, working with stakeholders across campus to support its international strategy. In addition to serving on various internal and external committees, Packer is the chair of the Canadian Bureau for International Education's Education Abroad Professional Learning Community and is a frequent presenter at both national and international conferences. She has an MEd in adult learning from the University of Calgary.

Joanna Regulska is vice provost and associate chancellor of global affairs and professor of gender, sexuality, and women's studies at the University of California, Davis. She has led transformative programs and partnerships for 30+ years. Two of the initiatives she currently leads are striving to provide all students with global learning experiences through Global Education for All, and strengthening research, education, and engagement efforts through Global Centers. A respected scholar, Regulska researches women's political activism, grassroots mobilization, decentralization, democracy, and democratization. She received her master's from University of Warsaw, Poland; doctorate from University of Colorado, Boulder; and doctor honoris causa from Tbilisi State University, Georgia.

Janaka Y. Ruwanpura is the vice provost international and a professor of engineering at the University of Calgary. Prior, he served as the director and Canada research chair in project management. Ruwanpura has been recognized for his outstanding academic, research, and administrative leadership with many local, national, and international awards. He led the University of Calgary to win five prestigious awards for internationalization and produced new models and tools to enhance internationalization. He is the current executive chair of the Commission on International Initiatives for the Association of Public and Land-grant Universities. He is a professional engineer and a professional quantity surveyor in Canada.

Jolynn Shoemaker is the director for global engagements at the University of California, Davis. Currently, she focuses on UC Davis engagement on the United Nations's Sustainable Development Goals, the UC Davis Global Centers, and other strategic initiatives. Previously, Shoemaker worked on international peace and security issues in Washington D.C., with a focus on gender equality. She has worked with nongovernmental organizations and served in both the U.S. Department of State and the U.S. Department of Defense. She holds a JD and an MA (School of Foreign Service) from Georgetown University and a BA from University of California, San Diego.

Shehan Thampapillai is the deputy director of international business intelligence and strategic planning at Central Queensland University in Australia. He has more than 17 years of experience in the international education field and has held numerous senior positions at higher education institutions in Australia and the United Kingdom.

Kalpen Trivedi is associate provost for international programs at the University of Massachusetts Amherst. Responsible for strategic and operational oversight of the International Programs Office, he also provides leadership for campus internationalization. Trivedi has 16 years of experience in international education, with special interest in program design, travel health and safety, and global partnerships. A regular contributor and presenter in various forums, he is former vice-chair and steering committee member of the Overseas Security Advisory Council's Academia Working Group, a member of the NAFSA Trainer Corps, and a member of The Guild of the College of Global Studies, Arcadia University.

Scott Vu is a partnerships officer on the Asia-Pacific team at the University of Calgary International. He helps facilitate international partnerships that accelerate the meaningful flow of knowledge, talent, and skills between Canada and the Asia-Pacific region. He holds a bachelor's of arts (co-op) in international relations, specializing in the Asia-Pacific region, from the University of Calgary. Vu was a member of the team that received the Canadian Bureau for International Education's Catalyst Award and the Association of International Education Administrators's Innovation Award for developing of the International Partnerships Assessment and Rating Index.

CPSIA information can be obtained
at www.ICGtesting.com
Printed in the USA
FSHW010445160520
70044FS